CHILDREN'S ACTIVITIES FOR THE CHRISTIAN YEAR

CHILDREN'S ACTIVITIES FOR THE CHRISTIAN YEAR

DELIA HALVERSON

ABINGDON PRESS
NASHVILLE

Library of Congress Cataloging-in-Publication Data

Halverson, Delia Touchton.
  Children's activities for the Christian year / Delia Halverson.
    p. cm.
  Includes index.
  ISBN 0-687-35233-9 (binding: adhesive, pbk.: alk. paper)
  1. Church year—Study and teaching (Elementary)—Activity programs. I. Title.
  BV30.H335 2004
  268'.432—dc22

2004005645

To my grandchildren
Jesse, Megan, Mya, and Lea

CONTENTS

As I write this I have renewed excitement about sharing the Christian seasons with children. My three- and seven-year-old grandchildren gleam with excitement over Christmas, and I have just met my infant twin granddaughters. What better way to introduce them to Christianity than through the cycle of seasons!

Children's Activities for the Christian Year will help you develop ways to use the seasons as tools to help children grow into disciples of Christ. The primary age for these activities is eight to twelve years, but there are many activities that can be used with younger children or in a mixed age group setting. On page 111 I have listed these activities as a quick reference along with suggestions for adapting the materials for younger children.

In the first chapter you will find helpful information about the establishment of the Christian seasons and the importance of rituals and symbols in our lives. The second chapter covers Sundays or "Mini-Easters" and will help children understand much of what we do when we celebrate worship each week. The next seven chapters carry you through the seasons beginning with Advent and ending with other special days that your church might celebrate.

At the beginning of each chapter you will find general information about the season and then a simple explanation that may be used with young children. Next is a section on symbols and colors of the season and then a variety of learning activities. Worship suggestions that may be used in a classroom or that are appropriate for home worship are also included. I offer suggestions on the next page on how to use some of these in corporate worship. Finally, each chapter includes reproducible sheets that are to be used with activities as indicated.

Although the primary audience of this book is the teacher in a classroom or small group setting (for example, children's church, children's groups, vacation Bible school, after school programs, and so forth), most of the suggestions are also appropriate for multiage home use. Be creative in the ways you share the seasons. Here are a few suggestions:

• Plan a common learning activity throughout the Sunday school to introduce each season. This will give children of different ages from the same home a shared experience.

• As you approach the season, design a special learning event that gives children an opportunity to experience the season in different ways. This might be on a Sunday afternoon or weekday evening. Set up several learning centers with activities and allow the children to choose ones of interest. This event can also be planned for families to experience together. If you expect a small group, set up several centers in a large room. If you expect a large group, set up each activity in a separate room and give families a description of each room's activity, allowing them to choose the ones they want to participate in.

• Use the materials in chapter 2 and design an event to help children (and parents, if you wish) learn about your worship area and corporate worship experience. Many parents do not recognize the symbols and meanings and are then at a loss to help their children understand them. This will provide them with common knowledge as they worship together as a family.

• Incorporate some of these ideas into a Bible retreat or other event centered on learning about the Bible. You might include:

• Plan a service project that is centered around a season. For example:

Whether you are working with a group of children or specific individuals, you will find joy in sharing the seasons with these young Christians.

The Christian seasons parallel the readings listed in the lectionary (see page 3), which many churches use in worship. It is important to include worship experiences, such as those I have suggested, in the classroom. It is also important for children to feel as though they are a part of the corporate worship experience, so consider including worship suggestions in your corporate worship services, where appropriate. For example, hymns and suggestions for visual imagery are listed for each season. These can be as effective for adults as they are for children and will give families a shared experience of a particular season.

• Use litanies that were created during class time during corporate worship.
• Use suggestions for Advent or Lenten wreaths (pages 19 and 56) and place them in the sanctuary.
• On Easter, bring the light into a dark sanctuary, as suggested on page 68.
• Use a variety of creeds in worship, including some created by the children.
• For All Saints' Day use the heritage bells suggested on page 102.
• Use the suggestions "Dedicate Items of Thankfulness" and "Offer Kernels of Thanks" on page 105 in a Thanksgiving corporate worship.

I hope that *Children's Activities for the Christian Year* provides the tools you need for sharing the joy of the Christian seasons. You will find that you will grow spiritually as you share these activities with children. As teachers of the faith, we often grow and learn even more than our students. If I can be of help to you, or if you would like to discuss any of these ideas further, feel free to contact me either through Abingdon Press or directly at:

Delia Halverson
915 Santa Anita Drive
Woodstock, GA 30189
770-926-1634
samandee2@cs.com

THE CHRISTIAN YEAR

By using the Christian year we relive the life of Christ each year and the impact that Christ's followers had, and are having, on the world. On the morning of the Resurrection, sorrow turned to joy, and the first day of the week became special to the disciples and friends of Jesus. They continued to worship with their religious Hebrew community, but a new layer of meaning had been added. To remember that additional meaning to life, the early Christians came together on every first day. The event of the Resurrection so affected their lives that early Christians began to celebrate the day each year. The celebrations of the Christian year began with what we presently call Easter. And so the weekly celebration of Sundays and the annual celebration of Christ's resurrection became the foundation of our current Christian calendar.

Christians of the third century held three-day celebrations of Jesus' death and resurrection during the time of Passover. This celebration has expanded to now include the whole of Holy Week. Many churches celebrate in some manner each day during that week, while others only celebrate on Palm Sunday, Maundy Thursday, and Good Friday, plus Easter Sunday.

The next celebration that the early church added to the church calendar was Pentecost, with an emphasis on the coming of the Holy Spirit and the celebration of Christ's ascension. The celebration of Epiphany came next, combining both Christ's birth and baptism. During this time Christianity was declared the official religion of the Roman world, and all citizens automatically became Christians. The specific celebration days for Christmas, Good Friday, and Ascension Day were then added, and by the end of the fourth century the basic pattern we observe today was established.

As the additional celebrations were added through the years, the richness of the seasons grew. Now we have a cycle, giving us opportunity to see the beginning with the end and to focus on the influence of Christ's life on our own.

TRADITIONS AND CELEBRATIONS

Traditions are very much a part of the lives of children. They even develop traditions about where to walk and what to step on or not step on!

How many children have you seen concentrate on either stepping on or avoiding the cracks in the sidewalk? I recall, as a child, always beginning a flight of stairs with my left foot because I felt that my left foot got neglected since I was right-handed.

Traditions can be both good and bad. They offer us stability in life. When there is a crisis, we often turn to a tradition for comfort, tying us to the life that we feel is stable. However, the tradition becomes unimportant after the crisis, if there is no connection to our everyday lives. If traditions get in the way of seeing life from our present perspective, then we need to take another look at them. Simply because something was done in a particular way at one time does not mean it should be done that way forever.

It is important that we have ownership in our traditions. We cannot appreciate a tradition that is forced upon us with no understanding of its meaning or no connection to our life. The advent of the contemporary service of worship illustrates this point. Over the years the Christian church developed rituals in worship that had meaning to those who planned and led in worship. But when church attendance became optional rather than expected, many younger members opted out because they were not taught the connection between the rituals and their own lives. As these folks realized a need for God in their lives, the contemporary service came into being, and with it new traditions were born, such as standing each time we sing and lifting our hands in prayer.

The Christian year is rich in traditions. These traditions bring certain things about the life of Christ or the mission of the church to mind. The cycle of the Christian year also brings stability to our year if we keep it connected with the core of our lives.

CYCLE OF SEASONS

This drawing is a graphic way to help us recognize the movement from one season to another.[1] Some Christian churches celebrate different dates for specific events because of differing calendars in the past and different ways of calculating the days. Some churches also emphasize one season more than another if it has meaning to that particular church.

By reliving the faith story each year, we reestablish its relevance to us, bringing a new understanding and influence on our lives. The seasons and the faith story will have new and different meanings for us next year, and the next, and the next as we grow and our lives change.

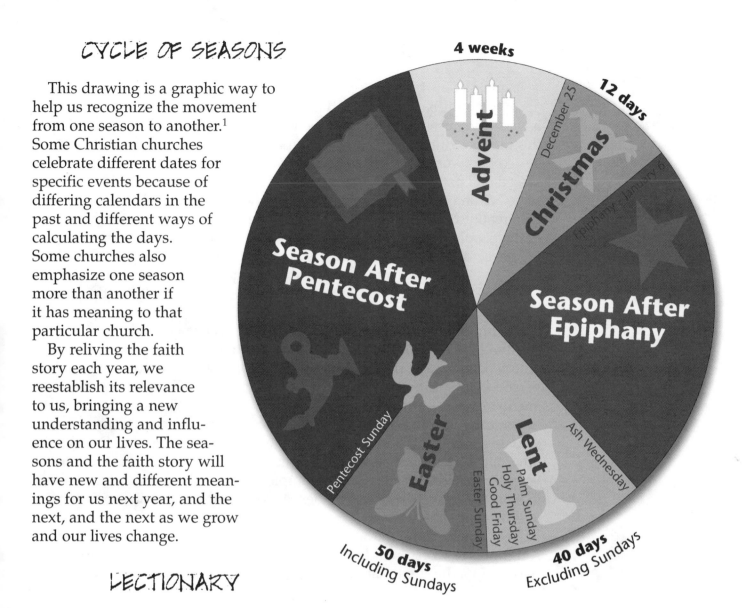

LECTIONARY

Recall the time when Jesus read in the synagogue (Luke 4:16-17) from a specific scroll that was given to him. Our practice of readings from a lectionary stems from the Hebrew custom of reading designated passages from the law and the prophets at specific times. Although use of the lectionary is optional, a larger number of churches follow it for a portion of the year as a means of moving through the cycle of the Christian year and covering most of the Bible.

The lectionary is an arrangement of scripture readings that are specific to certain Sundays and holy days. It moves us through the major parts of the Bible in a three-year plan (Years A, B, C). Each Sunday, readings are suggested from the Gospels, Epistles (letters), Old Testament, and Psalms. Seldom are all four passages read, but most churches using the lectionary will usually include at least two. The reading from the Psalms will often be in the form of a responsive reading.

THE WORK OF THE PEOPLE

There is a Greek word, *legitourgia* (which is made up of two words, *laos*, "people," and *ergon*, "work"), that forms the base for our word *liturgy*. It is a pattern for worship that is "the work of the people." Understanding this makes a difference in how we understand worship. It has been suggested that worship is not a spectator sport! Yet, at times, such emphasis is placed on "performance" that those leading worship feel that they are "on stage" to be viewed and approved of by the congregation.

In reality, quite the opposite is true if we recognize liturgy as the work of the people. Worship might be compared to a drama where the people are the actors, the worship leaders are the coaches, and God is the audience. The leaders are moving us, the congregation, to a true encounter with God. The liturgy should enable us to experience the Holy Spirit as alive and within us.

It is important, however, to recognize that every person does not grow spiritually in the same way. The liturgy that moves us to grow spiritually will depend greatly on our personalities. For instance, if you are a visual person your spiritual experience in worship may be hampered if there are no symbols or other visuals for you to focus on. These visuals do not necessarily need to be high tech in nature. In fact, sometimes this style of visual is distracting because it is often accompanied by audio. On the other hand, if you are someone needing audio input, the silence of some worship services may leave you completely cold. You, in fact, may be looking for opportunity to experience worship through music or other audio expressions.

As we move through the seasons, we need to recognize that each person comes to worship individually. As such, each will also interpret the seasons in a different manner.

4

SUNDAYS (MINI-EASTERS)

In the first story of creation in Genesis the writer speaks of God resting on the seventh day. The early Hebrew people patterned their lives in this fashion, working six days and resting on the seventh. Even during the early church, the followers of Jesus worshiped in the synagogues on the seventh day of the week. Because the Resurrection occurred on the first day of the week, they also celebrated each first day. As it became obvious that the Hebrew faith would not embrace Christ's followers, the celebration of the first day of the week became more prominent and the seventh-day celebration was dropped. These became "Mini-Easters," a time of remembering how our Lord conquered death.

It is significant that on the first day of creation God created light. The people of Rome dubbed the first day of the week *dies solis*, or "day of the sun," and soon Christians adopted the name and compared the rising of the sun to Christ's rising from the dead. The first day was declared as a day without work when Constantine, the emperor of Rome, became a Christian in the fourth century.

Finally, communion and baptism are most often celebrated on Sunday. The early Christians remembered the last supper that Jesus had with his disciples and used it as a connection with their resurrected Lord each time they met. Early Christianity required extensive study for those formally joining the faith, and the celebration of their uniting was also observed on Sunday. More detailed materials on communion are presented in chapter 6. More details on baptism can be found in chapter 5.

SIMPLE EXPLANATION

Sunday is the day that we set aside each week to worship God. In the Bible we read that after the creation God rested on the seventh day. The Hebrew people chose the seventh day as their day to rest and worship God. After Christ's resurrection on the first day of the week, Christians also celebrated that day as a "Mini-Easter," as a way of remembering him. Later they dropped the seventh-day celebration and simply concentrated on the first day. It is also interesting to remember that God created light on the first day of the week, and our Sunday worship helps us remember that Christ brought light, or new hope, to people who felt hopeless.

SYMBOLS AND COLORS

Colors: The color for each Sunday depends on the particular season in which it falls. However, if communion is not served each Sunday, then white is usually used on those Sundays when communion is served. White is also used for weddings and occasionally for baptisms. White signifies purity.

Symbols: You will find many symbols in your sanctuary or place of worship. Take children on a tour and explain those listed below and any others you find. Be sure to look at the architecture as well as the obvious and seasonal symbols that may be present. Is the room shaped like a cross? Look for arches and domes. Look for triangles, circles, and squares built into the architecture.

Cross	We remember that Christ died for us.
Candle	Christ is the light of the world.
Bible	The Bible is God's Word or guide.
Triangle/three circles	Anything in three parts reminds us that we experience God in three ways: as our creator/parent (Father), in human form (Son), and within us (Holy Spirit).
Circle	God's love is eternal, never ending.
Square (or four cornered object)	Four gospels.
Dome or arch	God's love surrounds us.
Stained glass windows	These were used when people could not read to remind them of the stories and symbols.
Raised area in front	We lift God above all else in our lives.

LEARNING ACTIVITIES

CREATE MUSICAL INSTRUMENTS

Rhythm Sticks—Use one-half- to one-inch dowels, cut in nine- to twelve-inch lengths. The sticks may be decorated with colored markers or paints. A coat of varnish will keep them bright. Use the sticks as instruments by hitting them together and/or on the floor.

Humming Comb—Cover a comb with wax paper. Hum into the teeth of the comb.

Drums—You may use various articles for drums, such as a round oatmeal box, a large commercial size can, the bottom of a large plastic jug, or unused paint cans or clay flower pots of graduating sizes. Bottles or glasses filled with different amounts of water create different tones when tapped lightly.

Shakers—Place small stones, buttons, or acorns between two aluminum pie tins or hard plastic cups. Tape the tins or cups together to make shakers. The items could also be placed in a box or covered can. Dried seed pods that rattle may also be used.

Wrist or Ankle Bells—Attach jingle bells to a band of one-inch elastic that will fit around a child's wrist or ankle. The bells may be sewn on or pinned to the elastic with large safety pins.

Sandblocks—Using two blocks of wood, about 2 x 4 x 4 inches, cut two pieces of coarse sandpaper about an inch larger and place them on one side of the blocks, folding the ends over the edge and tacking or stapling them securely. These are rubbed together to make a swishing sound.

Nail Triangles—Tie a short string to a large nail. Use another nail to strike the nail that is held with the string. This will produce a sound like the triangle.[1]

CREATE A CHORAL READING

This can be done using psalms or hymns. A choral reading is usually done antiphonally (first one group or individual and then another). Select phrases that lend heavier or darker feelings to be spoken by the deeper voices or the group as a whole, and use lighter phrases for individuals with higher voices. This is a tool for learning, not a performance. You may use the exact words from the Bible or paraphrase them, such as this one based on Psalm 100.[2]

Leader:	Sing praises to our God, everyone in the world!
Group 1:	Be joyful as you come to worship.
Group 2:	Come before God with happy songs!
Group 1:	You know that God is our God.
Voice 1:	God made us.
Voice 2:	We belong to God.
All:	**We are God's people, the sheep in God's pasture.**
Group 2:	Enter into God's house and give thanks.
Group 1:	Always give praise to God,
Group 2:	For God is good.
All:	**God's faithfulness lasts forever.**

LEARN HERITAGE PRAYERS AND CREEDS

There are many prayers and creeds from our heritage that we use in Sunday worship. Even when children do not yet understand exactly the concepts or words, it is important for them to learn to use them with the congregation. You might create a tape of your worship service with these prayers and creeds so that the children can learn to read with the congregation. Duplicate the tape for families to use in the car or at home.

CREATE A TIME LINE

Use the information at the beginning of this chapter to create a time line for the celebration of our Sundays.
Example:

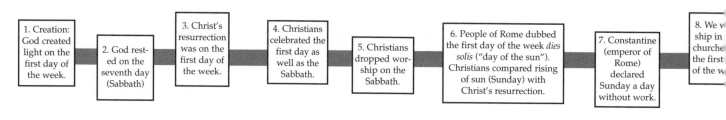

1. Creation: God created light on the first day of the week.

2. God rested on the seventh day (Sabbath)

3. Christ's resurrection was on the first day of the week.

4. Christians celebrated the first day as well as the Sabbath.

5. Christians dropped worship on the Sabbath.

6. People of Rome dubbed the first day of the week *dies solis* ("day of the sun"). Christians compared rising of sun (Sunday) with Christ's resurrection.

7. Constantine (emperor of Rome) declared Sunday a day without work.

8. We worship in churches the first [day] of the w[eek]

CREATE A BANNER

Use symbols of light to create a banner of the Lord's Day. The symbols may include candles, lamps, and sunrises. Get permission to display these in your place of worship for the whole congregation to enjoy.

MAKE A STAINED GLASS WINDOW

Remind the students that stained glass windows were first used when most people could not read. The windows reminded the worshipers of the stories and symbols of the faith. To make your own stained glass window, you will need:

- White paper (typing weight)
- Black construction paper
- Pencils, crayons, and scissors
- Black permanent marker
- Cooking oil
- Cotton swabs
- Plastic sheets and paper towels

Cut frames from the black construction paper, cutting out the space where the picture will show through. Place the frame over the paper and draw an outline of the opening where the picture will go.

Inside the open area, draw symbols or a picture outline with a pencil and trace over it with black permanent marker to represent the "leaded" part of the stained glass. Using crayons, color all parts inside the open area, including the background.

CHILDREN'S ACTIVITIES FOR THE CHRISTIAN YEAR

Use the plastic to protect the working surface; dip the cotton swabs in cooking oil and coat the back of the paper on the colored area. *Be careful not to use the oil outside the colored area where the frame will be glued.* Wipe away any excess oil with paper towels.

Glue the frame around the picture.

DO A CROSSWORD PUZZLE

See the reproducible sheet on page 10 for a crossword puzzle on "Those Who Help Us Worship." The answers are found on page 114.

WORSHIP SUGGESTIONS

USE VISUAL IMAGERY ON A CELEBRATION TABLE

Candle, lamp, or lantern to symbolize light (John 8:12)
Candle with a half-bushel basket placed beside it. (Matthew 5:15)

CREATE AND USE A LITANY

Use the reproducible on page 11 to create a litany for use in worship.

SING TOGETHER

Use hymns such as those listed below to remind the children that we celebrate Christ on the Lord's Day:

"Christ Is the World's Light"
"Come, Christians, Join to Sing"
"Morning Has Broken"
"Rise, Shine, You People"
"Shalom to You"
"This Is the Day"
"When Morning Gilds the Skies"

THOSE WHO HELP US WORSHIP

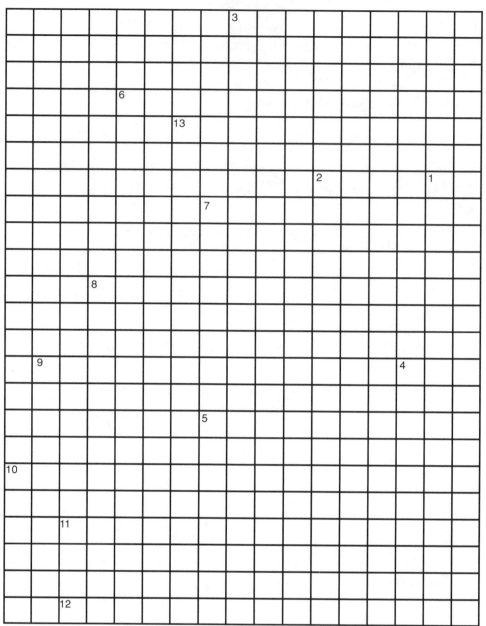

Down:

1. The person who preaches
2. The person who plays the organ
3. The person who leads us in our liturgy

4. People who take care of the altar area

5. Those who greet us at the door
6. The person who directs the music
9. Those who lead in worship by singing specials

Across:

7. The person who helps us find a seat
8. The band that plays songs of praise
9. The person who prepares communion
10. The team that leads us in songs of praise
11. Those who light candles and assist
12. The person who plays the piano
13. All of us who worship

Answers on page 114.

CREATE A LITANY

Create a litany to express feelings, to paraphrase scripture, or to praise God. In a litany the leader, or individual, reads leading statements, and the whole group responds. The response may always be the same or varied.

In the classroom, decide on the subject. If the response is to be the same each time, decide on that as a group. Assign smaller groups to develop a sentence about the subject (or to paraphrase sections of scripture). As you read the litany, the persons in each smaller group will respond with their sentence.

(Title) _____

Leader: _____

Response: _____

Group/person 1: _____

Response: _____

Group/person 2: _____

Response: _____

Group/person 3: _____

Response: _____

Group/person 4: _____

Response: _____

Group/person 5: _____

Response: _____

Group/person 6: _____

Response: _____

Leader: _____

Response: _____

REPRODUCIBLES

ADVENT AND CHRISTMAS

We consider Advent as the first in the cycle of Christian seasons. However, it was not the first to be celebrated since Jesus' followers believed that his return was to be immediate. Both Easter and Pentecost are closely related to Jewish holidays, so it was natural to associate those occasions with the Christian events and celebrate them.

Because Christmas provides a human aspect to the faith, it is an important celebration for children. Although they may not understand the divine aspect of the celebration, they can relate to a child born into a loving and common family, among animals, and in an obscure village.

The December date for the observance of Christ's birth may have originated as a celebration of the winter solstice in Rome. In fact, the dates of many of our Christian celebrations were originally pagan celebrations. Rather than fighting the pagan customs, the early Christians changed the celebrations to emphasize Christian heritage and ritual.

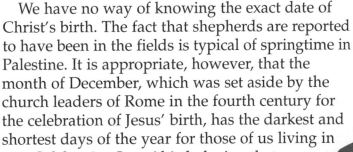

We have no way of knowing the exact date of Christ's birth. The fact that shepherds are reported to have been in the fields is typical of springtime in Palestine. It is appropriate, however, that the month of December, which was set aside by the church leaders of Rome in the fourth century for the celebration of Jesus' birth, has the darkest and shortest days of the year for those of us living in the Northern Hemisphere. Celebrating Jesus' birth during that month symbolizes Christ as the light coming into the world in the midst of darkness.

Originally, Advent was a period of penance and preparation for baptisms that took place on Epiphany (January 6). In the sixth century the celebration was moved to the four weeks prior to Christmas. Three centuries later the celebration became one of anticipation of Christ's coming, including the second coming of Christ.

We celebrate Advent beginning four Sundays before Christmas, and all of the days in between. The actual season of Christmas does not begin until Christmas Eve and lasts until Epiphany. Too often we consider the twelve days between Christmas Day and Epiphany to be "business as usual," as a time to recover from the flurry of pre-Christmas activities. So much emphasis is placed on receiving gifts on Christmas Day that, for the most part, the rest of the Christmas season is overlooked. Look for ways to help children live out their ministry through the Christmas season. Continue to wish people a merry Christmas season during that time, and don't hesitate to use activities to celebrate the birth of Christ. When a baby is born into a family, the celebration continues for weeks after the birth. This should hold true for the celebration of Christ's birth as well. Referring to December 25 as Christmas Day and the twelve days afterward as the Christmas season, will help children recognize this.

SIMPLE EXPLANATION

Advent is a time when we get ready to celebrate the birth of Jesus. It begins four Sundays before Christmas Day, so the exact date of the first day of Advent is different each year. This gives us four Sundays to really anticipate our great celebration. Although Christmas Day is celebrated on December 25, we do not know the exact date of Christ's birth. But it is appropriate that we celebrate this special birth during one of the darkest days of the year. This symbolizes the fact that Christ's birth brought new hope to a world that was depressed and did not see "light" or a way out of their "darkness." During Advent we think about the difference that Christ has made in the world.

The Christmas season begins on Christmas Eve and continues for twelve days after Christmas Day, ending on Epiphany, January 6. Just as we celebrate a child's birth after the actual date of birth, it is appropriate to celebrate Christ's birth for those additional twelve days.

SYMBOLS AND COLORS

Colors: The color most often used for Advent is purple, symbolizing the royalty of Christ. Blue is sometimes used since purple is also used for Lent. Blue symbolizes the hope that Christ brought to the world. We use white on Christmas Eve, Christmas Day, and until Epiphany to signify the purity of Christ. Gold is also used during the Christmas season, symbolizing the royalty of Christ.

Symbols: Advent and Christmas symbols are popular because Christmas cards use many of them. Most symbols, such as those listed below, are used during both Advent and Christmas seasons.

Angel	Angels told of Christ's birth.
Bells	Celebrate Christ's coming.
Candles	Christ is a light to a dark world.
Evergreens	God's love is everlasting.

Manger	Christ's birth is for all people.
Trumpets	Herald Christ's coming.
Wreath	God's love is eternal.

LEARNING ACTIVITIES

MAKE A JESSE TREE

Create a Jesse tree to celebrate the heritage of Jesus (Isaiah 11:1). The following scriptures and symbols are common ones to hang on the Jesse tree.[1]

Abraham	Genesis 15:1-6	Star
Sarah	Genesis 21:1-8	Baby
Isaac	Genesis 22:1-14	Altar
Rebecca	Genesis 24:12-20	Water jug
Jacob	Genesis 28:1-22	Stairway
Rachel	Genesis 29:15-20	Number 7
Joseph	Genesis 37:1-4	Coat
Judah	Genesis 37:25-28	Coins
Joseph	Genesis 44:1-17	Cup
Ruth	Ruth 2:1-12	Wheat
Boaz	Ruth 4	Sandal
Jesse	1 Samuel 16:1-13	Sheep
David	2 Samuel 2:1-7	Crown
Solomon	1 Kings 3:1-15	Gavel
Jehoshaphat	2 Chronicles 20:1-12	Praying hands
Hezekiah	2 Chronicles 29:1-11	Gates to Temple
Josiah	2 Kings 22:8-20	Scroll
Joseph	Matthew 1:18-25	Angel
Mary	Luke 2:1-7	Manger
Jesus	Matthew 3:13-17	Dove

DO A CROSSWORD PUZZLE

See the reproducible on page 21 for a crossword puzzle on "Colors and Symbols of Advent and Christmas." The answers are found on page 114.

LEARN CHRISTMAS CAROLS AND STORIES

Learn the Christmas carols on pages 23-24 and share the stories behind them.

FOLLOW A DAYSPRING MAZE

Ask the children for suggestions of what the word *dayspring* might mean. (*Spring* indicates a new beginning, and *day* indicates light conquering

darkness.) Follow the maze on page 22 together, finding the scripture indicated. After you have finished, ask how the coming of Christ has made a difference in the world.

RESEARCH VARIOUS CUSTOMS

Research various customs associated with Christmas and Advent in other countries. Check out www.christmas.com/worldview/ for Christmas customs around the world.

MAKE AN ALUMINUM CAN LANTERN

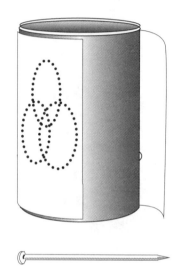

You will need:

- tin cans filled with frozen water
- hammer and large nails
- paper to fit around cans (may use back side of labels)
- tape and pencil
- gloss black spray paint
- votive candle

Draw designs on the paper, such as stars, crosses, and other Christmas symbols. Tape the paper to the can and pound nails along the design lines, through the can and into the block of ice. The more holes you insert the more light you will have. When the design is complete, remove the paper and the ice and dry the can thoroughly. Spray the can with gloss black paint. Place a votive candle inside. You may attach a wire bail for hanging.

CELEBRATE HERITAGE

Invite children to bring bells to decorate a tree. Each bell will be placed on the tree in honor or in memory of someone who has helped them to know God better. Use Exodus 28:33-35 and the hymn "I Heard the Bells on Christmas Day." Henry Wadsworth Longfellow wrote this hymn in 1863 after he was saddened by the Civil War, in which his only son was seriously wounded.

LEARN ABOUT ST. NICHOLAS

Nicholas was a young boy who loved Jesus and tried to help others by performing kind deeds without letting anyone know who did them. Later he became a bishop, and people remember him today as a saint because that's what we call people who love God. Check the library and internet (www.christmas.com/worldview/) for the full story.

CREATE A MONOLOGUE

Enter the classroom telling the story from the viewpoint of a prophet, innkeeper, shepherd, Joseph, Mary, Simeon, or Anna.

FOLLOW A MAP

Use a map of Palestine to trace the likely route that Mary and Joseph took from Nazareth to Jerusalem (see page 45). The custom of the Jews then was to cross the Jordan River north of Samaria and come back across the river south of that country because the Samaritans were thought to be unclean. Talk about how, as an adult, Jesus spoke favorably of the Samaritans. (Luke 10:25-37; John 4:1-26)

MAKE AN ADVENT CHAIN

Using the suggestions on the "Giving Tree" on page 25, make a chain of twenty-four links. The chain is put together, and then, as each suggestion is carried out, the link is removed until there are no links left at Christmas.

PREPARE THE MANGER

Give each child a box that can be used as the "manger" and a small bag of straw. Tell them to add a straw to the manger each time they do a kind act. Their goal is to prepare a soft bed for the Baby Jesus before Christmas.

MAKE A TREE OF GIFTS

Set up an artificial tree and ask children to bring specific gifts for a mission project. The gifts may be mittens, scarves, caps, toiletries, and so on. Select a destination for the gifts and deliver them.

CREATE A CHRISTMAS SHOP

Stock it with gifts that the children can purchase for a predetermined charity. After a child purchases a gift, provide wrapping paper so that it can be wrapped and later delivered. Set a cost limit for the price of the gifts.

LEARN "THE TWELVE DAYS OF CHRISTMAS"

This song may have originally been used to teach Christianity. Write the following words from the song on 3 x 5 inch cards with the meaning of the words on the reverse side. Randomly distribute the cards and then ask the children to stand in order according to their cards. You may want to sing the song as you arrange the order. Then ask each child, in order, to share the meaning on the backs of their cards.

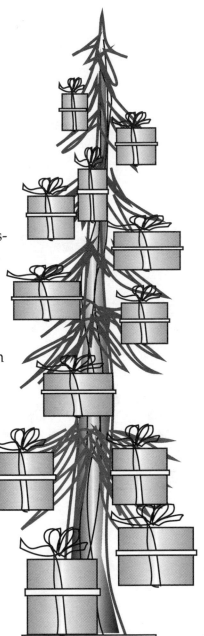

True Love	God
Me	Baptized Christian
Partridge in pear tree	Jesus (A partridge acts as decoy to save her babies.)
Two turtle doves	Old and New Testaments, witnesses of God

Three French hens	Faith, Hope, Love (1 Corinthians 13:13)
Four calling birds	Four Gospels (Matthew, Mark, Luke, John)
Five gold rings	Torah (first five books of the Old Testament)
Six geese a-laying	Six days that God created (Genesis 1)
Seven swans a-swimming	Seven gifts of the Holy Spirit (Romans 12:6-8 and 1 Corinthians 12:8-11)
Eight maids a-milking	Eight Beatitudes (Matthew 5:3-10)
Nine ladies dancing	Nine fruits of the Holy Spirit (Galatians 5:22)
Ten lords a-leaping	Ten Commandments (Exodus 20:1-7)
Eleven pipers piping	Eleven faithful apostles (minus Judas Iscariot)
Twelve drummers drumming	Twelve points in the Apostles' Creed

STUDY THE NATIVITY IN DIFFERENT CULTURES

Help children recognize that people can relate to the Christmas story better if the Nativity reflects their culture. Assemble pictures of the nativity from different nationalities. You may also find that the members of your church have Nativity sets that depict different cultures. Invite them to bring their sets and display them for the children to see. Remind the children that although the sets are different, each carries the same theme, that Christ came into the world.

GIVE EVERGREEN FOR LOVE

Give children sprigs of evergreen as a symbol that God's love is forever and does not die. Or, if available, get small evergreen trees and give one to each child or family.

EXPERIENCE CHRISTMAS IN A BARN

There are several options for experiencing the joy of Christ's birth in a barn.

Visit a farm and enjoy the animals. Then move to the barn and dramatize the birth story in the barn setting, much like the stable where Jesus was born.

Make a trip around town looking for the true meaning of Christmas. On the trip you may see persons doing acts of kindness, Nativity scenes, hospitals where persons are helping the sick, and so on. Finally end up at a farm where a bright light is shining through the barn door. Enter the barn to find the scene of Jesus' birth.

Tell the children that you are going on a mystery trip. Just before arriving at the farm, stop and blindfold the children. Ask them what it feels like to be in darkness and if they would like to have light. Assist them out of the car, each holding hands with another, forming a chain. Lead them into the barn and tell them to take off their blindfolds. At the moment they remove their blindfold, turn a spotlight or large flashlight onto the scene of Jesus' birth.

CREATE A GIVING TREE

Use the reproducible on page 25 to help children find ways to share God's love during each day of Advent. They will select one item to do each day and color in that part of the Advent calendar. By Christmas it will be complete.

WORSHIP SUGGESTIONS

USE VISUAL IMAGERY

Use the imagery from one of the lists below, one for each Sunday of Advent and Christmas Eve or Christmas Day.

1st Sunday	Hope	Star
2nd Sunday	Faith	Cross
3rd Sunday	Joy	Bell
4th Sunday	Love	Heart
Christmas (Eve)	Peace	Dove

Use crèche
1st Sunday	Prepare (Isaiah 11:1-2)	Straw in stable
2nd Sunday	Journey (Luke 2:1-5)	Mary and Joseph added
3rd Sunday	Birth (Luke 2:6-7)	Baby Jesus
4th Sunday	Listen (Luke 2:8-20)	Angel and shepherds
Christmas (Eve)	Spread news (Matthew 2:1-12)	Wise men at a distance

To prepare means to get to know something well. This use of scriptures helps the child know the story ahead of time. Note that the wise men are kept at a distance because they did not come until later, when the family had moved into a house.

LIGHT AN ADVENT WREATH

Use an Advent wreath with four purple candles and one white (Christ) candle in the middle. Read the following scriptures each Sunday of Advent as you light one additional candle. The final center candle is lit on Christmas Eve or Christmas Day.

Anticipation	Isaiah 11:1-2
Announcement	Luke 1:26-35
Affirmation	Isaiah 62:10-12
Arrival	Luke 2:1-7
Appreciation (white candle)	Luke 2:8-20

CREATE A CHORAL READING

Use Isaiah 9:6 as a choral reading. Write the words on newsprint and first read all of the words together. Then divide the verse, having the girls

---

and boys read different sections. When you reach the different names for Jesus (Wonderful Counselor, Mighty God, and so on) assign one word to a different person.

SING TOGETHER

Use carols such as those listed on the reproducible on pages 23-24 and remind the children that during Advent and Christmas we celebrate Christ coming to this world. You might also sing "Come, Thou Long-Expected Jesus" during Advent.

COLORS AND SYMBOLS OF ADVENT AND CHRISTMAS

Answers on page 114.

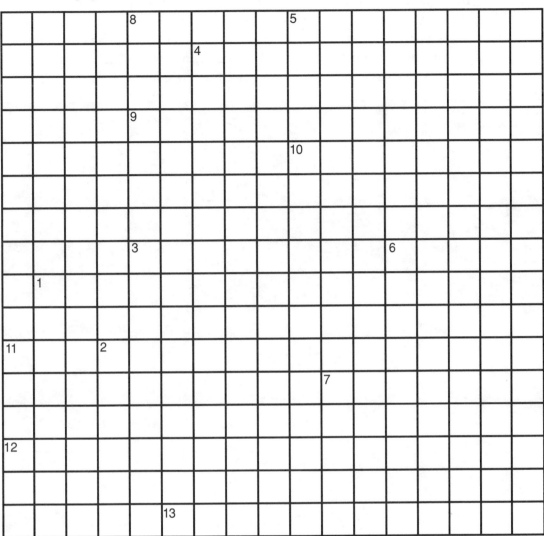

Down:
1. The bright light that shone over Bethlehem
2. A bird that symbolizes peace
3. Something we ring to celebrate Christ's birth
4. Instruments to herald Christ's coming
5. Green tree: God's everlasting love
6. Place where Baby Jesus lay
7. Color: purity
8. Place where Jesus was born

Across:
3. City where Jesus was born
7. Circle of greens: God's love never ends
9. Color symbolizing hope
10. Bright color: Christ's royalty
11. A light: Christ is the light of the world
12. Heavenly being: told Mary of birth
13. Rich color: Christ's royalty

DAYSPRING MAZE

Begin at the lower left and follow the maze to find the Dayspring. Along the way you will find times when the Hebrew people felt that life was hardly worth living. Visit those areas and read about their problems, but then return to the main path and make your way to the Dayspring that we call Christmas, the birth of Christ the Messiah.

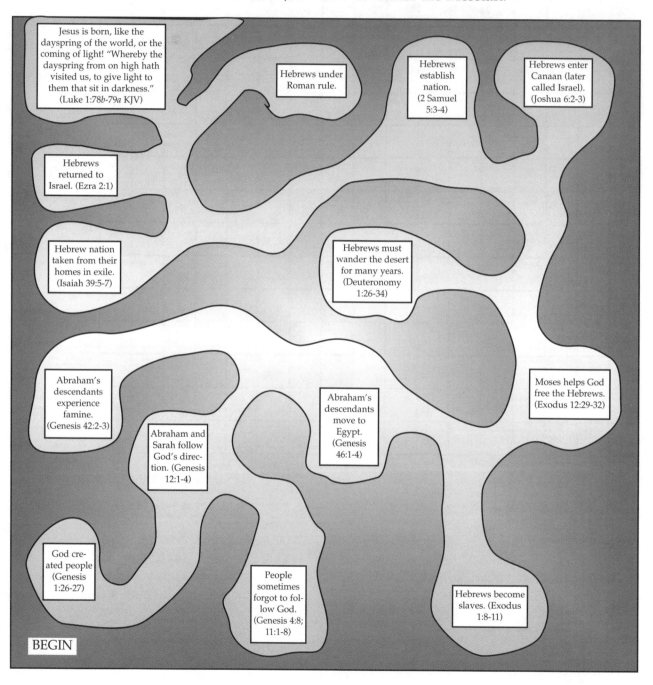

CHRISTMAS CAROL STORIES

The word *carol* comes from the word carole or a ring dance. The dance was accompanied by singing. Some carols are folk songs that have had words added to them. There is a legend that St. Francis of Assisi originated caroling. He also is credited with making the Nativity scene popular in order to help the villagers experience the Scriptures. The custom of singing as they strolled through the village may be the foundation for our caroling from door to door.

"O Little Town of Bethlehem"

Phillips Brooks, an Episcopal minister, made a trip to the Holy Land in 1865. On Christmas Eve he rode a horse out to Bethlehem. The scene of the village in the distance impressed him so that when he returned to his home in Philadelphia he wrote the words for the children in his church to recite. He asked the church organist, Lewis Redner, to compose music. It was not until the middle of the night before the performance that the music came to his mind.

"O Come, All Ye Faithful"

The writer of this carol was not known until over two hundred years after it was written when an old manuscript was discovered. An Englishman, John Wade, was living in France when he wrote the words in 1744. The monks in France chanted it as they marched in a procession to church on Christmas Eve. This chanting became known as "Midnight Mass."

"While Shepherds Watched Their Flocks by Night"

This song comes from Luke 2:8-11 and was written more than three hundred years ago by Nahum Tate, one of the best known Irish poets of his time. This is his most popular contribution.

"Away in a Manger"

Martin Luther is often given the credit for writing this carol, but there is no evidence of exactly who wrote it. The German Lutherans brought the carol to America where it was first printed in 1885 in Pennsylvania. Then it was printed in England and later in Germany where it must have originated. The third verse was written later.

"We Three Kings"

An Episcopal pastor, John Henry Hopkins Jr., wrote both the words and music for this carol in 1857. It is considered the first all-American

carol. It is one of the few carols that mentions the wise men. Note that the scripture does not call them kings and does not specify exactly how many wise men there were (Matthew 2:1-12). We usually speak of three wise men because of the three gifts they brought.

"HARK! THE HERALD ANGELS SING"

In 1739 Charles Wesley wrote this carol, although it was not sung to the same tune that we use today. One hundred years later Felix Mendelssohn, a famous musician, wrote the music. Charles Wesley wrote more than six thousand hymns in his lifetime.

"SILENT NIGHT"

Joseph Mohr, a Catholic priest in an Austrian village, wrote these words in 1818. In 1820, when the organ could not be used because the mice had chewed holes in the bellows, his organist, Franz Gruber, set the poem to music so that it could be sung on Christmas Eve with a guitar. For many years the names of those who wrote this carol were not known.

"JOY TO THE WORLD"

Rumor says that Isaac Watts complained that the church songs were not joyful enough, and after a challenge from his parents he wrote this song. It was not actually written as a Christmas carol. Watts has been called the father of English hymnody. He published 52 volumes of hymns and songs. This carol is based on Psalm 98.

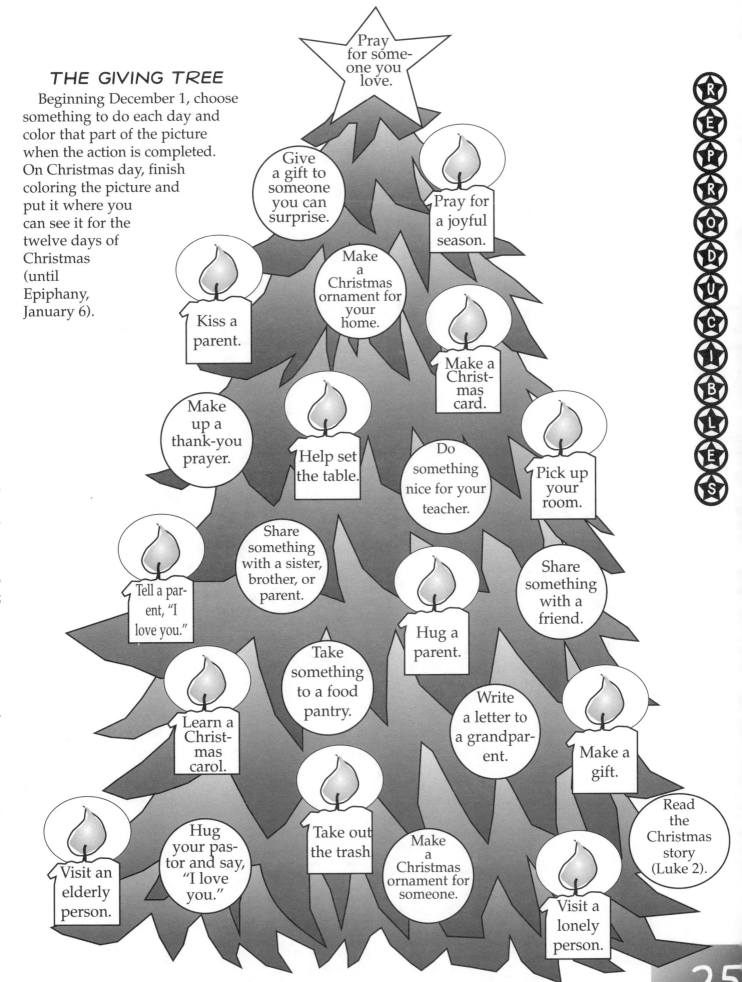

THE GIVING TREE

Beginning December 1, choose something to do each day and color that part of the picture when the action is completed. On Christmas day, finish coloring the picture and put it where you can see it for the twelve days of Christmas (until Epiphany, January 6).

Pray for someone you love.

Give a gift to someone you can surprise.

Pray for a joyful season.

Make a Christmas ornament for your home.

Kiss a parent.

Make a Christmas card.

Make up a thank-you prayer.

Help set the table.

Do something nice for your teacher.

Pick up your room.

Tell a parent, "I love you."

Share something with a sister, brother, or parent.

Hug a parent.

Share something with a friend.

Learn a Christmas carol.

Take something to a food pantry.

Write a letter to a grandparent.

Make a gift.

Visit an elderly person.

Hug your pastor and say, "I love you."

Take out the trash.

Make a Christmas ornament for someone.

Read the Christmas story (Luke 2).

Visit a lonely person.

R E P R O D U C I B L E S

25

EPIPHANY

Epiphany, as we celebrate it on January 6, means "to appear or manifest." The wise men went forth to search for the Christ Child, God's manifestation on earth. After finding him, they went forth to spread the good news to other countries. We have many misconceptions about this story. Traditionally, we call these travelers wise men. The Greek word used for these travelers is *magi*, which is not a literal translation of the word kings, as is commonly believed. It appears, however, that they were astrologers, probably from Persia. We usually speak of three wise men, but the only indication that there were three men is the three gifts they left. No number is mentioned in the text.

We also think of the wise men as coming to the stable, where the shepherds found the Christ Child. However, the text specifically states, "On entering the house." Herod's decree for the death of children under two years of age also indicates that time had elapsed between the sighting of the star and their arrival, making the Christ Child somewhat older than an infant.

When we celebrate Epiphany today, we emphasize two things: the fact that Christ came for all people, even those beyond the national boundaries of Palestine, and the importance of spreading the news of Christ's birth. Older children can recognize the importance of sharing the good news with others, no matter where they live.

SIMPLE EXPLANATION

Epiphany, which means "to appear," is celebrated on January 6, or the twelfth day after Christmas Day. If it does not fall on a Sunday, it is sometimes celebrated on the following Sunday. Epiphany is when we remember the wise men who went forth looking for the "child who has been born king of the Jews" and then went home to spread the word. The Bible does not tell us how many men there were, only that there were three gifts.

SYMBOLS AND COLORS

Color: The color for Epiphany is green, symbolizing the growth or spread of Christ throughout the world as the wise men carried the message back to their homes.

Symbols:

Crowns	Wise men's visit
Star	Wise men's sign of the birth
Three gifts	The gifts of the wise men

LEARNING ACTIVITIES

MAKE LUMINARIAS

Use a small plain paper bag. Turn the top down about two inches to form a cuff. Draw and cut out a star shape on one side of the bag and punch small holes in all other sides of the bag. Fill the bottom of the bag with sand or dirt and set a candle in the sand. When the candle is lit the light shines through the holes. Place the luminarias outside to guide the way.

ACT OUT A STORY

Use a one- or two-year-old child as Jesus and as many magi as necessary to be sure each child has a part. Using an older child instead of an infant reminds us that the wise men came after Jesus was older, and the numerous wise men remind us that we do not know just how many magi there were.

REVIEW THE TWELVE DAYS OF CHRISTMAS

Epiphany climaxes the twelve days of the Christmas season. Review the original meaning of the poem and song "The Twelve Days of Christmas" that appears on pages 17-18.

EXCHANGE GIFTS

We give one another gifts to remember how the wise men brought gifts to the Christ Child in exchange for God's gift to the world. Exchange gifts in a unique way by having everyone leave their gifts in a basket and remove one shoe at the door. Then, while everyone is playing a game, someone distributes the gifts, placing one in each shoe. The shoe with its gift is then matched with its owner. This is reminiscent of the custom in parts of Mexico and Europe where shoes are left outside the door to receive gifts from the wise men.

Make a "Love Gifts" Bulletin Board or Poster

As you think about the gifts that the wise men brought to Jesus, create a bulletin board of the gifts of love that we bring to Christ—gifts that cannot be wrapped. Ask children to illustrate these gifts for the bulletin board or a poster.

Collect for a Food Pantry

Decorate a large box as a wrapped gift and collect food items for the food pantry. As you share with others, remember that Jesus was born in poor circumstances.

Research Wise Men's Trip

Provide resources for research on the conditions of travel at the time of Jesus' birth, such as the care of camels, star locations, traveling conditions, and food that was taken and eaten on trips. Help the children research and then make up a might-have-been story about the trip that the wise men would have taken. They may want to act out the story or dress up in costume and travel to another classroom to tell the story.

Play a Board Game

Divide the class into groups of four or less to play the game. Hand out the reproducible on page 33, "Journey with the Wise Men," and be sure that they understand the directions.

Arrange the Camels

Cut fifteen camels out of construction paper and on each camel attach a section of the story found on the reproducible sheet on page 34. Hand out the camels in random order. Then ask the children to arrange themselves according to the story. When they are in place, ask each child to read his or her part of the story in order. (If you do not have fifteen children, simply work as a group to arrange the camels on the floor.)

Learn about Customs in Other Countries

Churches in many parts of the world consider Epiphany more important than Christmas:
In Lithuania, the evenings between Christmas Day and Epiphany are

called holy evenings, and Epiphany becomes a time for feasting, dancing, and singing.

In France, friends and family gather on Epiphany for the traditional feast.

In Ireland, Epiphany is called the Feast of the Three Kings or Little Christmas. Some families celebrate with a special afternoon tea and a late night feast. They place a candle on the cake for each family member present.

In Mexico, children anxiously await January 6 when they wake up to find toys and gifts left by the *Reyes Magos* (Magi). In some regions it is customary for children to leave their shoes out so that the visiting wise men can leave treasures in them.

In some South American countries, bales of hay are left outside the door for the camels of the wise men.

MAKE AN OUTREACH TREE

To emphasize the theme of Epiphany—that Christ came for all the earth—make an outreach tree. Stand a large bare branch in a pail of sand. Make large green construction paper leaves for the tree and on each leaf place a picture and information about an outreach or mission project of your church. You may also use symbols and miniatures (as found in craft stores for dollhouses) to depict these ministries. Talk about the way your church shares God's love with others.

TAKE A DIFFERENT ROUTE HOME

Ask families to return home using a different route, as the wise men returned using a different route to protect the identity of the Christ Child.

WORSHIP SUGGESTIONS

LEAD THE WISE MEN

As you begin your worship time, have persons dressed as wise men come out of the group and ask, "Have you seen the child that was supposed to be born?" As the teacher or leader, you will reply, "Will you come with me?" then you will lead them and the children to the worship area for worship.

USE AN IRISH BLESSING

Use the reproducible on page 32 to use an Irish blessing.

SING TOGETHER

Use hymns such as those listed on the next page and remind the children of the theme of Epiphany, that Christ's message is for the whole world.

"Blest Be the Tie That Binds"
"Christ for the World We Sing"
"God Be with You till We Meet Again"
"Heralds of Christ"
"In Christ There Is No East or West"
"Joy to the World"
"Love Came Down at Christmas"
"O Come, All Ye Faithful" (verse 1)
"O Little Town of Bethlehem"
"The First Noel"
"We Three Kings"

An Irish Blessing

God bless the corners of your house
and all the lintels blessed.
And bless the hearth, and bless the board,
and bless each place of rest.
And bless each door that opens wide
to strangers as to kin,
And bless each crystal window pane
that lets the starlight in,
And bless the rooftop overhead,
and every sturdy wall.
The peace of man. The peace of God.
With peace and love for all.

Irish Christmas Blessing

JOURNEY WITH THE WISE MEN (MATTHEW 2:1-12)

START
You see the star and know that the king of the Jews has been born.

Go ahead 1 space. Others agree to join you. (The Bible does not record the number.)

Go back 2 spaces. You forget to get gifts for the king.

Go ahead 2 spaces. You also choose incense and myrrh.

Go ahead 1 space. You choose to take gold for the king.

Go back 4 spaces. In Jerusalem you meet King Herod, but you are not impressed.

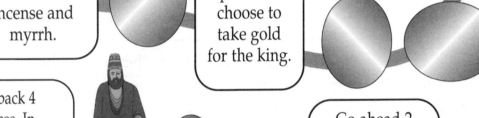

Go ahead 2 spaces. Scribes tell you the king is to be born in Bethlehem.

You greet the Christ Child and give him your gifts. Then you return home by a different route.

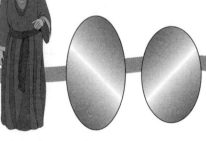

Go ahead 1 space. You see the star over a house in Bethlehem.

Go back 2 spaces. You lost the road.

DIRECTIONS:
Select a marker for each player.
Cut 5 small squares of paper the same size, numbering them 1-5. Mix them up and place in a box.
Draw a number. Highest number plays first. (If more than 5 play, each draws a number and puts it back.)
In turn, draw a number and move marker that number of spaces. Return number to box.
Draw and play until all players complete game.

Permission to photocopy this handout granted for local church organization use only. Reproduced from Delia Halverson, *Children's Activities for the Christian Year*. Copyright © 2004 by Abingdon Press.

33

ARRANGE THE CAMELS

	Jesus was born in Bethlehem in Judea during the time of King Herod.
	Wise men in the East saw the star.
	The wise men traveled many days from the East to Judea.
	The wise men stopped in Jerusalem and asked King Herod where the king of the Jews was born.
	The chief priests and teachers of the law said the prophet wrote that the child was to be born in Bethlehem.
	Herod told the wise men to report back to him when they found the king child.
	The wise men went to Bethlehem.
	The star stopped over the place where the child was.
	The wise men went into the house and bowed down and worshiped him.
	The wise men gave treasured gifts to Jesus.
	Warned by a dream, the wise men returned home by a different route.
	God warned Joseph in a dream to take the child and his mother and go to Egypt.
	Herod was furious that the wise men hadn't returned, so he ordered all of the boys in the Bethlehem area who were two years old and under to be killed.
	Joseph and Mary and the baby stayed in Egypt until King Herod died.
	Matthew 2:1-20

SEASON AFTER EPIPHANY (ORDINARY TIME)

CHAPTER 5

"Ordinary time" comes twice in our Christian calendar: immediately following Epiphany and the time between Pentecost and Advent. The word *ordinary*, in this case, has no reference to "common" or "mundane." This comes from the word *ordinal*, which simply means "counted" or "chronological time." This is time in order.

The season after Epiphany is a good time to emphasize the life and teachings of Jesus. We have just celebrated his birth, and now we begin the process of marking the time of his life. Another emphasis during this time might be spreading the gospel to all parts of the world as we follow the example of the wise men.

In our world it is easy to concentrate on activities that provide glitzy children's programs and that compete with the neighboring churches for a bigger and more elaborate children's ministry program. In reality though, giving children a firm foundation in the stories of Jesus is of prime importance. Ordinary time is a good opportunity to concentrate on these stories of Jesus' life. Children learn best by repetition, so do not hesitate to repeat stories. Each time the story is repeated consider using different learning activities to reinforce their learning experience and help children with different learning styles also become familiar with the stories. As you enjoy the stories, speak of how these are the stories of the adult Jesus whose birth we celebrated at Christmas. It is important for children to see the connection between the baby Jesus of Christmas and the adult Jesus who helped us to better understand God. This is also a good time to explore the meaning of baptism, linking it with the baptism of Jesus. No matter what style of baptism your church uses, it is important that children learn about the various types of baptism, particularly in your own church setting. Acknowledge the legitimacy of each church's tradition and explain why your church celebrates the sacrament in a specific manner.

Instead of letting this season fall between the cracks because it does not include a major celebration day, make use of ordinary time to stretch the children's minds about Jesus' life and his influence on the world.

SIMPLE EXPLANATION

Just like any of us, Jesus grew from childhood to adulthood. During the season after Epiphany we think about all that Jesus did during his adult life. We think about the stories he told and about the people he knew and helped. Sometimes we call this season "ordinary time" because it is time in order. This is the arranged time of Jesus' life. It is also a good time to think about how the message of Jesus has spread through the world, much like the wise men who took the message of Jesus' birth back to their country.

SYMBOLS AND COLORS

Color: Green is the color used for the ordinary time after Epiphany, as well as the ordinary time after Pentecost. For Epiphany, this color signifies the growth of Christ and his ministry as he became a man.

Symbols:

Dove	Christ's baptism
Shell	Christ's baptism
Fish	Christ's call to disciples
Lamp	Christ is the light of the world
Loaves and fishes	Christ fed the multitude as well as ministered to others in need
Shepherd	Christ as shepherd
Chi Rho (ky-row)	First two letters in Greek word for Christ, placed together

LEARNING ACTIVITIES

BAPTISM

Because Jesus began his ministry with baptism, this is a good time to look at the understanding of this sacrament. The sacraments (sacred moments) help us to taste, touch, feel, know, and experience the special love (grace) of God. Communion is discussed along with Holy Week in chapter 6.

Do a Crossword Puzzle

Use the reproducible crossword puzzle on page 44 to learn about baptism. Have children work in pairs. When they have filled in all they can, discuss all the answers so that all of the puzzle is complete. The answers are found on page 114.

Make a Collage of Water

Divide a large piece of paper into three sections. Label the sections:

- Water gives life.
- Water cleanses us.
- Water refreshes us.

Search magazines for pictures of water that represent these three aspects. Glue the pictures in these three sections. When the collage is complete talk about how these three aspects of water and baptism are similar.

Discuss Methods of Baptism

Ask the children about baptisms that they have observed. As they tell about these events, recognize the methods of baptism that were used. The most common will probably be to sprinkle. Explain the three methods that many churches use:

Sprinkling	spreading God's love
Pouring	symbolic of the pouring out of the Holy Spirit
Immersion	cleansing of our sins to start anew

Explain to the children that churches that baptize infants believe it is a way that we come into the family of God. Parents take certain vows to raise the child in the Christian faith, and the congregation usually vows to assist the parents in this. Children who are baptized as infants have the opportunity to confirm these vows when they later accept them for themselves. Many churches call this "confirmation."

Make Baptism Story Walks

First read the story of Jesus' baptism (Matthew 3:13-17). Ask the children to work in groups of four and write, in simple language, the story

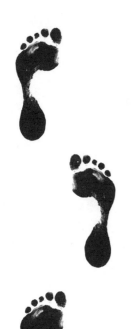

themselves. Have each group read their story. Then have each group divide their story into short phrases that will fit on a construction paper footprint. The footprints will be made by drawing around a shoe. They will be laid out in a left/right fashion, and the phrases are then written on each footprint in order. Use masking tape to tape the footprints on the floor so that as you step on the footprints you can read the story. Place these story walks at various points around the church for others to enjoy.

ENJOY SHELLS

Spend some time looking at various types of shells, recalling that the shell (usually a scallop shell) is a symbol of baptism. Compare the shells. Even if they are the same type, each shell varies in color and composition somewhat. Remember that God also made each of us as individuals, none exactly alike.

MAKE A BAPTISM GIFT

Make a gift to be given at a future baptism. You might decorate an infant blanket or crib sheet (or pillow case for an older child). Use pictures of water and shells or write messages from each person. Do this with permanent markers or fabric crayons (that are ironed in) and wash the article before presenting it as a gift.

JESUS' LIFE AND TEACHINGS

We find it easy to tell the stories of Jesus, but this time should also help us grasp some of the attitudes that Jesus had about life and relationships.

IMAGERY OF JESUS' LIFE

Use a guided imagery to tell a story from Jesus' life. Use the following as a starting point for the story of the sower and seeds.

You are walking on a hot and dusty road in Galilee when the wind brings a scent of water. You look up, and in the distance you see a hint of blue. It must be the Sea of Galilee! As you come closer, you realize that there is a crowd gathered on the shore of the lake. There is a man sitting in a boat close to shore. The crowd had pressed so close to him that the only way he could have more room was to get into the boat. But wait. As you get closer you realize that the man is talking, and everyone is listening, even the young children. He's telling a story. Listen:

A farmer went out to scatter seed in a field. While the farmer was scattering the seed, some of it fell along the road and was eaten by birds. Other seeds fell on thin, rocky ground and quickly started growing because the soil wasn't very deep. But when the sun came up, the plants were scorched and dried up, because they did not have enough roots. Some other seeds fell where thornbushes grew up and choked the plants. But a few seeds did fall on good ground where the plants produced a hundred or sixty or thirty times as much as was scattered. If you have ears, pay attention! (Matthew 13:3-9 CEV)

The man said, "If you have ears, pay attention!" Does that mean it's something you should think about? Think about what this means.

Monologues

This is a great time to create monologues. Either have adults develop a monologue and come into the classroom, or help the children develop a monologue themselves by reading the story, learning about the circumstances and customs of the era, and even dressing in costume to be a character from the story remembering what happened or as a bystander recalling their observation of the action. In a monologue you can include feelings that the person might have had and incidental things that might have happened at the time. The key phrase here is "might have happened." The story not only includes the biblical text but also helps the children become a part of the scene by expanding the ideas of what might have happened at the time.

"I Am" Statements

Jesus made several "I am" statements. These may be studied and illustrated in several ways. You might use them for banners, poetry, booklets, songs, or even a video or PowerPoint presentation.

John 6:35	Bread
John 8:12	Light
John 10:7	Gate
John 10:11-14	Good shepherd
John 11:25-26	Resurrection and life
John 14:6	Way
John 15:1	Vine

Remember that "I am" is the name God told Moses to use (Exodus 3:1-14).

DRAWING AND PAINTING

Artistic ways of illustrating the stories of Jesus can include murals, greeting cards, comic books (see below), and basic drawing and painting. Older children respond better to drawing and painting when there is an end purpose, such as making a book for a younger class or illustrating a poster to share with the whole church.

COMIC BOOKS

This is a good tool for middle and older elementary children. After sharing the story, plan as a group just what scenes will be used to make the story complete. Where possible, allow the children to choose the scenes they will draw and then assign scenes not chosen. After the scenes are completed, use a copy machine to reduce them in size and place them in sequence of four to six on a page. Make enough copies for each person. Copies may be colored with crayons and placed in the church library or other classrooms.

STORY BLOCK

Either use a box or make a cube from poster-weight paper or cardboard, using the reproducible on page 43. Enlarge the pattern to at least three inches square. Decide what scenes will illustrate the life of Jesus (or an individual story) and draw those on the squares. You may use six scenes, or use five and place the name of the story on the sixth space on the block. After the cube is put together, it may be used to review the life of Jesus or to retell a particular story.[1]

DRAMA

There are many ways to use drama to help children remember the life of Jesus. Here are a few:

- spontaneously act out the scenes as a story is told
- use the game of charades to remember a story
- make and use puppets
- act as a reporter interviewing someone who was with Jesus
- create play readings (for example, parts are read instead of memorized, and very few if any props are used) using words directly from the scripture or making up the script yourself
- role play by taking the story to the point of the solution and then asking the children to fill in the solution

WRITING

Writing can be dull or exciting, depending on how it is approached. When the writing places the child in the position of a character in the story, it becomes much more exciting.

- Make a newspaper, creating articles centering around weather, traveling conditions, political activity, police activity, local economic conditions, as well as news reporting.
- Make a résumé for Jesus. This would include information about his life, his career as a carpenter, his career as an itinerant preacher, and might even have information about his personal goals.
- Create poetry telling the story of Jesus' life. Try an acrostic poem where the first letter of each line forms a word when read vertically.

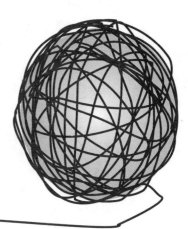

MAP MAKING

Use a map to review Jesus' life and teachings. Use the basic reproducible map on page 45 to locate the places of specific activities in Jesus' life.

STORY WEB

Using a ball of string or yarn is a good way to tell or review a story. Divide the story into different sections, assigning the sections to different children. It is best if each person in the group has an assigned section. If the group is too large, ask those with assigned sections to space themselves around the circle. The person assigned to the first section of the story holds the ball of yarn. After telling the assigned part of the story, he or she holds the end of the yarn and then rolls the yarn ball across the circle to the person with the next assigned part of the story, unwinding the yarn. That person tells the next part of the story and holds onto part of the yarn (or wraps it around the wrist) and rolls the ball across to the next person, and so on until the complete story is told, weaving a web across the circle.

DISCIPLE SONG

There are several songs that list the names of the disciples, or you can sing the following words to the tune of the children's song "Oats, Peas, Beans, and Barley Grow."[2]

Pe-ter, John, and two named James,
An-drew, Mat-thew, Phi-lip too.
Tho-mas, Si-mon, Bar-thol-o-mew,
And Ju-das one and Ju-das two.

WORSHIP SUGGESTIONS

USE VISUAL IMAGERY

This might include fish and fishnets (symbolizing any time in Jesus' life when he spoke of fishing or was fishing with his friends); water, shells, dove (symbolizing Jesus' baptism); stones, seeds, pearl, coins, sheep, and other items (representing the parables); lamps or candles (representing Christ as the light of the world).

REMEMBER BAPTISM

Stand in a circle and, as you all sing "We Are the Church," take a bowl with water from person to person and ask them to lift a handful of water and let it trickle through their fingers, remembering their own baptism or the baptism of another person.

CREATE AND USE A LITANY

Create a litany about water and how it relates to baptism, or about the life of Jesus. You may use responses such as: "Thank you, God, for your gift of baptism" or "And Jesus grew and told others about God."

SING TOGETHER

Use hymns such as those listed below that tell us something about baptism.

> "A Charge to Keep I Have"
> "Child of Blessing, Child of Promise"
> "Here I Am, Lord"
> "I Have Decided to Follow Jesus"
> "Let There Be Peace on Earth"
> "Take My Life, and Let It Be"

Use hymns like the ones listed below to celebrate the life of Jesus.

> "Fairest Lord Jesus"
> "Jesus' Hands Were Kind Hands"
> "O Young and Fearless Prophet"
> "Tell Me the Stories of Jesus"
> "We Would See Jesus"

STORY BLOCK

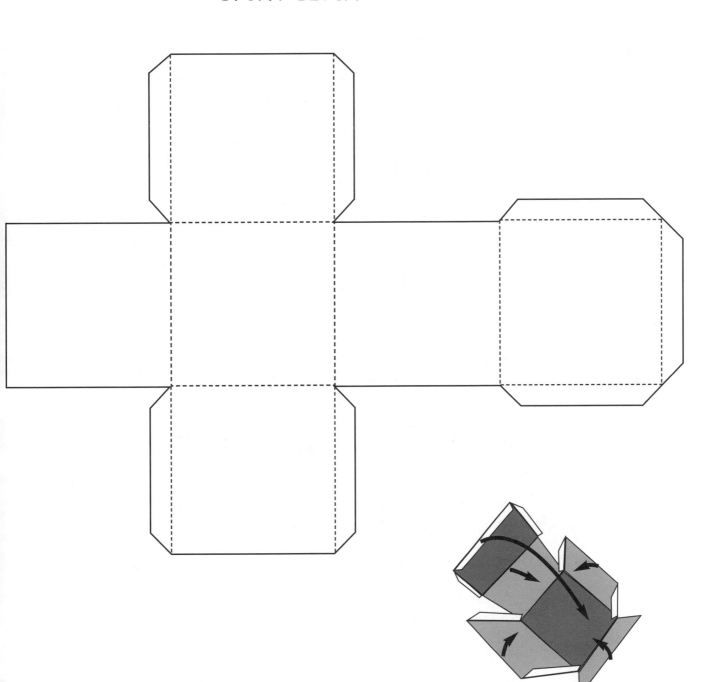

Draw your scenes on the block. Cut out along solid lines. Fold on dotted lines. Fold tabs under and tape or glue.

REPRODUCIBLES

BAPTISM

Answers on page 114.

Down:

1. When a baby is baptized, parents _ _ _ _ _ _ _ to teach the child about God.
2. During baptism, _ _ _ _ _ reminds us that Christ makes us clean of our wrongdoings.
3. Jesus' baptism was in the _ _ _ _ _ _ River.
4. Many churches use a baptismal _ _ _ _ to hold the water for baptism.
5. Besides baptism, another sacrament is _ _ _ _ _ _ _ _ _.
6. Besides communion, another sacrament is _ _ _ _ _ _ _.
7. One way to baptize is to _ _ _ _ _ _ _ _ water on the head.
8. A symbol of baptism that can be found in the ocean is a _ _ _ _ _.

Across:

4. When we are baptized as adults we ask God for _ _ _ _ _ _ _ _ _ _ _ for our wrongdoings.
9. One way to baptize is to _ _ _ _ water over the head.
10. One way to baptize is to _ _ _ _ _ _ _ the person in the water.
11. Water during baptism can make us feel _ _ _ _ _.
12. Baptism and Communion are both _ _ _ _ _ _ _ _ _ _, which means "sacred moments."
13. Jesus' cousin who baptized him was named _ _ _ _.
14. Another word for God's love that we feel at baptism is _ _ _ _ _.

Permission to photocopy this handout granted for local church organization use only. Reproduced from Delia Halverson, *Children's Activities for the Christian Year*. Copyright © 2004 by Abingdon Press.

REPRODUCIBLES

44

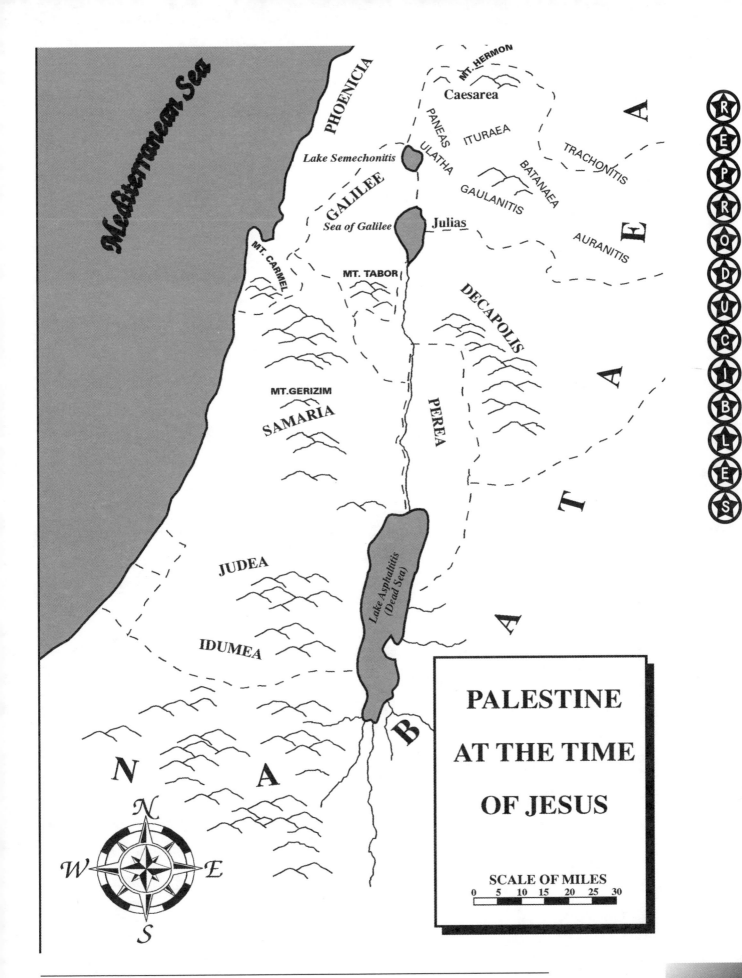

PALESTINE AT THE TIME OF JESUS

SCALE OF MILES

0 5 10 15 20 25 30

ASH WEDNESDAY, LENT, AND HOLY WEEK

The forty-day preparation period before Easter is our season of Lent. The forty days do not include Sundays, which are considered "Mini-Easters" or "feast days." The first day of Lent is Ash Wednesday when we begin our preparation for Easter. In many churches an Ash Wednesday service includes the tradition of placing ashes on the forehead in the sign of the cross, reminding us of our mortality (that is, our return to ashes) and our Christian belief of eternal life (that is, the cross).

The number forty is a number that is used to represent fullness—the amount of time needed to accomplish a specific purpose. It rained for forty days and forty nights; the Israelites wandered for forty years; Moses was on the mountain for forty days (twice); several kings ruled for forty years each; the Hebrews were exiled for forty years; Jesus fasted for forty days in the wilderness; and after the Resurrection, Jesus was revealed to the disciples for a forty-day period. In the early church, new converts were given forty days of preparation before being baptized on Easter Sunday.

Forty days is a long period for children. You may find that they have difficulty understanding that we need forty days to alter habits or patterns. Consider dividing the time into smaller increments, which are easier for children to understand and deal with. It may also be easier to focus on the positive, by helping the children decide to do something positive during the time instead of "giving up" something, which has a negative connotation.

Holy Week is a part of Lent. The various aspects of Holy Week offer numerous teaching opportunities and could provide a whole month of learning activities by itself. One option for including more of these activities is to use a few of the Holy Week activities before the actual week begins. For example, Palm Sunday reminds us of the entrance that Jesus made when he rode into Jerusalem on a donkey. Kings at war rode into a city on a horse, but when they came in peace they rode a donkey.

Maundy Thursday is an important part of Holy Week. The word *Maundy* comes from the Latin word *mandatum*, which is the root of our

word *mandate*. After the Passover meal with his disciples, Christ commanded (mandated) them to love one another so that they would be known as his disciples.

According to the Jewish custom of counting days from sunset to sunset, the actual arrest of Jesus came on Friday. Then after the mockery of a trial, Jesus was crucified. It is important, with children, to emphasize that Jesus' enemies brought about his death, not the Jewish people. It is also important to always follow up any story of Jesus' death with the statement that "God would not let Jesus stay dead." This is why we have an Easter morning. With younger children, we refer to the cross as a reminder of God's love in a special way. Elementary children can recognize the cross as a symbol that tells us that God's love is far greater than any wrong we may do. Older elementary children may recognize that Jesus could have avoided the cross because God has given humans a free will, but Jesus stood firm in his beliefs about God.

SIMPLE EXPLANATION

Lent is a forty-day period before Easter when we prepare ourselves. During that time we remember Christ and the change that he made in the world, and we try to better ourselves as followers of Christ. Many people follow the custom of "giving up" something during Lent to remind them of Christ's suffering. Some people decide to make some sort of change in their lives during this time in order to be a better follower of Christ.

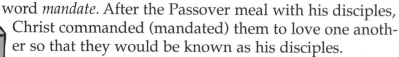

SYMBOLS AND COLORS OF LENT

AND EASTERTIDE

The symbols and colors for both Lent and Eastertide are included here because we use many of them for both seasons.

Colors:

Lent	purple	penitence
Eastertide	white	purity

Symbols:

Ashes	Our mortality, sorrow, and repentance
Basin and towel	Jesus washing feet at Last Supper, servanthood
Bread and cup	Christ's body and blood and the last supper he had with disciples
Butterfly	Chrysalis represents tomb, and butterfly the Resurrection

Cock	Reminds us of Peter's denial and warns us to be loyal to Christ
Coins	Judas's betrayal of Christ
Cross (empty)	Christ's resurrection
Crown of thorns	Christ's suffering and humiliation
Crucifix	Christ's sacrifice on cross
Donkey	Jesus rode into Jerusalem on Palm Sunday on a donkey.
Dogwood	Blossom in form of cross, legend that dogwood was a tall and straight tree until used as Jesus' cross
Easter lily	The bulb that appears to be dead comes to life.
Egg	Symbolizes renewal of life and resurrection. In early days, eggs were only dyed red to symbolize the blood of Christ.
Fish	Greek letters for fish are first letters in "Jesus Christ, Son of God, Savior." Jesus told us to be "fishers of people."
Lamb	Lambs were used for sacrifice. Christ sacrificed his life for us.
Lantern	Soldiers used lanterns and torches when they arrested Jesus.
Light	Christ's triumph over darkness (death)
Nails	Nails driven into Jesus' hands and feet
Palms	Jesus' ride into Jerusalem
Passion flower	Five stamen represent five wounds; rays represent halo and divinity; leaf is shaped like a spear.
Pelican	Legend of pelican piercing breast with beak to feed young in times of crisis. Pelican catches fish, and Jesus told us to be "fishers of people."
Robe and dice	Soldiers gambled over Jesus' robe.
Rope	Used to bind Jesus
Sand dollar	Four holes on shell represent four nail holes in Christ's hands and feet and larger hole represents spear hole. On one side is the design of an Easter lily. The bones inside center of sand dollar are in the shape of doves.
Seed	What appears dead comes to life.
Stone	The stone over the door of the tomb that was rolled away

LEARNING ACTIVITIES

SET A PATTERN

The forty days of Lent is a good time for children to set a pattern for doing something positive. Talk about acts of kindness that they might do during those days to help other people. Copy the reproducible on page 54 and have them fill in the pledge. There are forty spaces to record the acts of kindness as they carry them out. After Easter, discuss how successful they were and whether it made them more conscious of just what they could do for others.

DO A CROSSWORD PUZZLE

See the reproducible on page 58 for a crossword puzzle on "Colors and Symbols of Lent and Easter." The answers are found on page 115.

DO A WORD SEARCH

Use the word search reproducible on pages 60-61 to help the children realize why we use forty days for Lent. The answers are found on page 115.

PLANT A TREE

Planting a live tree offers an opportunity to remember that Christ's death and resurrection points to eternal life. You might place a cross beside the tree during Lent to remind us of the tree that Christ died on. If there is no room for planting a tree in your church yard, consider a park or the private home of a member of your congregation. If you would like to give a live tree to each child to plant in his or her own yard, contact your county extension agent for information on purchasing them at a nominal fee.

HOLD A PAX CAKE SERVICE

During the tenth century, in England, it became a tradition during Lent to serve *pax* cakes. The word *pax* is Latin for "peace." These are small pancakes. You can create an observance by suggesting that the children forgive someone (such as a member of their family or a friend with whom they have quarreled) or that they repent of some negative thought or act they have committed. Remind the child that when we forgive, we have peace with that person.

MAKE WAXED ONIONS

Like the symbol of eggs, onions give an appearance of no life, yet they do contain life that sprouts. Both of these can be symbols of the

Resurrection. Sprouting onions that are coated with a colored wax can last up to six weeks if kept out of the sun or a direct source of heat. To do this, select onions that are beginning to sprout. Place cans (vegetable- or fruit-can size) of colored wax (use several crayons in the wax for color) in a pan of boiling water. You may use water in an old electric fry pan for the cans. Dip the onions into the liquid wax several times to reach the desired hue. Do not leave the onions in the wax very long or the previous coats of wax will melt. After Easter the sprouts may be cut off and used in a salad and the wax broken from the bulb. The bulb will have shriveled, but it usually will still produce another bulb if planted outside.

USE THE SENSES

Use some of the following suggestions during Lent to help children relate to the experiences that Christ went through.[1] All five senses are used in these experiences.

Favorite hymn	Mark 14:26	They sang a song and went out. Remember familiar Lenten and Easter songs.
Strip of leather	John 18:12-14	Wrap leather around wrists and imagine how it must have felt.
Thorn or thorny branch	Mark 15:16-20	Feel thorn, remembering the pain Christ endured because he would not go against his beliefs.
Rough wood or piece of bark	Luke 23:26	Feel the bark and remember the man who carried the cross for Jesus, Simon of Cyrene. Consider how he felt with that responsibility.
Spike or large nail	John 19:16-18	During silence, have someone pound nail and then imagine how it must have been to hear the nails being pounded into Christ's hands and feet.
Cotton swab	Mark 15:23	Dip a cotton swab in a bowl of vinegar and taste it, remembering that Jesus felt the pain for us instead of taking a painkiller used in that day.
Small bag of spices	Mark 16:1-8	As you smell the spices, remember how women took spices to the tomb to cover the smell of the decaying body they expected to find.
Candle	2 Corinthians 4:4	The candle brings light to darkness, as Christ brought eternal light to a dark world.

FORCE BUDS

Bring barren branches inside and place them in water, forcing them to bud early. Be sure that these are branches where you can see small buds already formed. Forsythia is ideal for this. The buds remind us of how our faith grows through nourishment during Lent.

MAKE PRETZELS

Pretzels were first formed to remind us of hands and arms folded in prayer. First known by their Latin name, *bracellae*, or "little arms," the name then became *bretzel* and now *pretzel*.

- Mix 1 packet (1 teaspoon) yeast and ¾ cup warm water.
- Add 1 Tablespoon sugar, 1 Tablespoon oil, and ½ teaspoon salt.
- Mix in 2 cups plain flour.
- Knead and form into pretzels, folding ends over in praying formation.
- Place on foil and brush tops with beaten egg; sprinkle with coarse salt.
- Bake 10 minutes at 425°.

EXPLORE FEELINGS

Using the reproducible on pages 62-63, ask children to look up the scripture and fill in how Jesus might have felt in the particular situations. You may want to have the children work in teams as they look up the scripture, but encourage them to think for themselves about the possible feelings and fill in their own thoughts. A list of possible feelings is provided at the end of the reproducible, but you are not limited to using those words on the list.

WRITE "I WONDER" LETTERS TO GOD

These give children the opportunity to think through some questions they may have about life and about faith. Encourage them to simply write the letters as if they are talking to God. Then tell them that their letters are a form of prayer during this Lenten season.

DISCUSS FASTING

After reading Matthew 6:16-18 talk about how fasting helps us remember how Jesus suffered and how other people suffer today. Encourage the children to plan to give up something for a period of time or to forgo a meal at their favorite restaurant and give the money to a mission.

Research Crosses

Look at the Internet and other resources and learn about different styles of crosses and the meaning behind them. Ask members of your congregation to bring various crosses for a display that everyone can enjoy.

Have a Seder Meal

Use items below to enjoy a meal of remembrance like the one that Jesus shared with his disciples at Passover. The meal is a way of remembering when Moses led the Hebrew slaves out of Egypt. They reclined at the table at this meal because they were free people.

Matzo (flat bread)—Hebrews had to leave quickly and did not have time for the bread to rise.

Bitter herb (parsley)—Similar to hyssop, the brush-like plant used to paint the door posts with the blood of the lamb. Bitterness also reminds us of the bitter treatment of the Hebrew slaves.

Salt water (to dip herb)—Remembering the tears of the Hebrews in slavery. Also a reminder of the Sea of Reeds that they crossed.

Lamb bone—Reminder of the lamb sacrificed at the first Passover.

Egg—Represents life of firstborn who was saved by God when the Egyptian firstborn sons were killed.

Haroset (kha-row-SET)—This mixture of chopped apples, nuts, and cinnamon reminds us of the clay of the bricks the Hebrews had to make as slaves.

Make Matzo

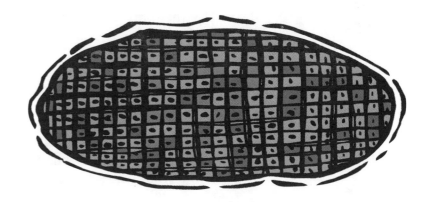

4 cups flour
1 tablespoon salt
2 tablespoons cold butter or margarine
1 cup cold water
Pastry cutter or two table knives
5-inch glass or coffee can
2 cookie sheets

- Mix the flour and salt.
- Add the butter or margarine and mix it with a pastry cutter or two table knives until it resembles coarse meal.
- Add the water and mix. Knead the dough for 10 minutes.
- Roll very thin and cut into five-inch circles with a glass or coffee can. (Should make about 12 circles.)
- Place circles on a greased cookie sheet. Place another cookie sheet directly on top of the circles to keep them from curling.
- Bake at 375° for 20 minutes. Remove and cool on wire rack.

Recall that the Hebrews had to leave Egypt quickly and could not let their bread rise, so they ate flat bread. When they celebrate their release from slavery, they eat Matzo and thank God.

MAKE A FINGER LABYRINTH

A labyrinth is a tool for meditation. These were first placed on the floors of medieval churches in Europe, and people walked the path focusing on God and scriptures as they walked. Since Lent is a specific time when we pray and renew our faith, invite children to use their fingers to "walk" the labyrinth on the reproducible on page 64. Suggest that they use the time to pray, to reflect on what's happening in their lives, to focus on some question about God, to remember scripture, or simply to quiet themselves.

PASS THE LIGHT

The Greek Orthodox have a tradition called Phos (meaning light) where one person carries the light home from church and then it is passed from house to house during Lent. You can do this with children in a class or among families who wish to participate. Purchase a large purple or white candle and carve a cross in one side of it. Make a list of those who wish to participate. The first family uses the candle for one day and then passes it on to the next, and they to the next on down the line. When the candle has made the circle, begin over again and continue the rotation throughout Lent. The candle then is brought back to the church on Easter.

USE A LENTEN CALENDAR

Use the reproducible on page 59 for children to follow each day of Lent.

MAKE A PRAYER JOURNAL

Lent is a good time to talk with God in a journal fashion. Encourage children to journal at home, or you might provide the journals for the beginning of a class session, telling them that no one will read their journal, although they may share their writings with people as they like. Make journal pages for children to use by heading them:

- When I've seen God in another person's life
- When I've felt God was urging me to do a loving act
- When I've seen God in nature
- Persons I want to pray for during Lent
- Times I've tried to act as a better person
- Some things I need to avoid doing during Lent
- Just talking to God about anything

REVIEW THE DISCIPLES' STORY

Use the following scriptures for various "disciples" to tell part of the story.[2] Questions leading into the monologues are also suggested.

PERSON	LEADING QUESTION	SCRIPTURE
John	John, will you tell us about the meal you and the other disciples had with Jesus the night before he died?	Luke 22:7-13
Peter	Jesus performed a common act before the meal. Peter, will you tell us about that?	John 13:2-17
Nathaniel	Nathaniel, will you tell us about how Jesus predicted that Judas would betray him?	Matthew 26:20-25
Andrew	Andrew, weren't you at the supper? Please tell us about how Jesus used the bread and wine to remind us of him.	1 Corinthians 11:23-26
James	James, can you tell us what happened next?	Matthew 26:36-46
Peter	Peter, when you were in the garden, some soldiers came for Jesus. What happened then?	John 18:2-14
Thomas	Thomas, will you tell us about the trial of Jesus?	Luke 23:1-25
Matthew	Matthew, you later wrote about how the soldiers mocked Jesus. Will you tell us about it?	Matthew 27:27-31
John	John, you were at the foot of the cross. Will you tell us about the crucifixion?	John 19:16b-30

CREATE A HOLY WEEK TIMELINE

Use the following scripture to create a timeline for Holy Week: Matthew 21:12-13; Matthew 26:6-7; Luke 19:30-40; Luke 19:41-44; Mark 14:32-42; Luke 22:15; Matthew 26:47-56; Matthew 26:57-65; Matthew 27:11-31; Matthew 27:33-55; and Matthew 28:1-10.

WORSHIP SUGGESTIONS

MAKE A LENTEN WREATH

This wreath is similar to the Advent wreath, but you may want to use pink and purple ribbons to decorate it. Use five purple candles, one pink (for Palm Sunday), and one large white candle (for Easter). On the first Sunday light all candles and during the meditation extinguish one purple one. On the second Sunday light all candles and extinguish two, and so on until Easter when they are all lit and remain lit.

USE VISUAL IMAGERY

Consider: basin and towel (*service to others*), road or path (*our way to the cross*), icons of Christ, praying hands (*preparing through prayer*). During Holy Week use palms and blankets for Palm Sunday, bread and cup or grapes and wheat for Maundy Thursday, and a hammer and spikes or old fence post with rusted spikes in it for reflection on Good Friday.

MAKE A CROWN OF THORNS

Provide garden gloves and invite children to work with thorny vines, making a crown of thorns. Then use the crown on the celebration table, and during the worship pass the crown around among the children as you sing one of the crucifixion songs listed below. You might arrange for the crown of thorns to be used in your congregational worship.

SING TOGETHER

Use hymns such as those listed and remind the children that we re-member to ask forgiveness for our sins and to remember Jesus' last days.

"Jesus Walked This Lonesome Valley"
"We Sang Our Glad Hosannas"
Ash Wednesday:
"Change My Heart, O God"
"Into My Heart"
"Sunday's Palms Are Wednesday's Ashes"
Palm Sunday:
"Hosanna! Hosanna!"
Last Supper:
"Broken for Me"
"Eat This Bread"
"Fill My Cup, Lord"
"Let Us Break Bread Together"
"One Bread, One Body"
Crucifixion:
"O, How He Loves You and Me"
"Were You There?"

LENTEN PLEDGE

I know that there are times when I could be more caring of others. During this forty-day peri-od of Lent, I pledge to find some act of kindness each day that will show God's love to another person. By doing this for forty days I expect it to become a habit to look for ways to be kind. I will keep track of these acts of kindness in the chart below.

Signed _____ Date _____

1	2	3	4
5	6	7	8
9	10	11	12
13	14	15	16
17	18	19	20
21	22	23	24
25	26	27	28
29	30	31	32
33	34	35	36
37	38	39	40

Now it is a habit! I will try to continue to find acts of kindness to do for others.

Signed _____ Date _____

COLORS AND SYMBOLS OF LENT AND EASTER

Down:
1. Animal Jesus rode on
2. Color: purity
3. Instrument of Jesus' death
4. Insect that seems dead but comes to life
5. Items from Jesus' last meal with disciples
6. Items thrown in roadway when Jesus came
7. Used to put Jesus on the cross
8. Reminds us of Peter's denial
9. Reminds us Jesus sacrificed for us

Across:
8. Reminds us Judas betrayed Jesus
10. Rolled from tomb on Easter
11. Placed on Jesus' head at trial
12. A plant that seems dead but sprouts life
13. Appears dead but live animal emerges
14. Represent servanthood—Jesus washed feet
15. Color: used on Good Friday
16. Color: symbolizing penitence

Answers on page 115.

LENTEN CALENDAR

Select a way to practice Lent each day and color in the square when you have completed the act. When Easter comes, you will have a colorful calendar and many memories.

Make a book about Holy Week for your family or a friend.	Color eggs, remembering that the shell can symbolize Christ's tomb.	Make a collage of pictures of flowers for Easter.	Make a food treat for someone who is sick or in a nursing home.	Write a poem about one day during Holy Week.	Share a special worship service with your family or friends.
Go through your clothing and toys and give some away to others.	Tell someone why you celebrate Lent.	Thank a teacher for helping you learn.	Check a book about Easter out of the library and share it with your family.	Make an Easter card for someone.	Pray for people who are fighting in the world.
Write a message of love for each member of your family.	Pray for someone you love.		Pray for someone who is ill.	Say your own prayer at a meal.	Don't complain for twenty-four hours.
Prepare dates and nuts for your family.	Run an errand for an older person.	Pray for people without a job.		Spend fifteen minutes in silence, just listening to God.	Hug each person in your family *real good*!
Read about Jesus entering Jerusalem. (Matthew 21:1-11)	Pray for doctors and nurses.		Hug a pastor.	Draw a picture of different types of crosses.	Give everyone you meet a smile today.
Read the Easter story from the Bible. (John 20:1-10)	Draw a picture of the crucifixion or Easter. (Mark 15:22-41)	Pray for families who don't live together.	Pray for your nearest neighbor.	Give a parent a hug.	Take some food items to a food pantry.
Write a letter to someone.	Bake a special bread for your family and remember the Last Supper.	Clean your room to prepare for Easter.	Help a sister or a brother or a younger friend.	Help wash windows to prepare for Easter.	Pray for those who are hungry in the world today.
Read about the Last Supper. (Mark 14:12-25)	Plant a bulb and watch it sprout.	Read the crucifixion story from the Bible.	Visit a lonely person.	Make hot cross buns.	Read about Jesus' praying in the garden. (Luke 22:39-46)

REPRODUCIBLES

FORTY DAYS

There are many times in the Bible when the time frame involved the number forty. In biblical times, the number forty was assigned to the time necessary for accomplishment.

Fill in the blanks below and find and circle the missing words in the word search puzzle. You may use the Bible references to help find the words.

1. The _ _ _ _ fell on Noah's _ _ _ for forty days. (Genesis 8:6)
2. Isaac was forty years old when he married _ _ _ _ _ _ _. (Genesis 25:20)
3. Forty days was the required time for embalming when Israel _ _ _ _. (Genesis 50:3)
4. Moses was forty years old when he killed an Egyptian and fled to Midian. Forty years later he experienced God in the _ _ _ _ _ _ _ bush. (Acts 7:23-30)
5. The Israelites ate _ _ _ _ _ for forty years in the wilderness before entering the promised land. (Exodus 16:35)
6. Twice Moses was on the _ _ _ _ _ _ _ _ for forty days and forty nights. (Exodus 24:18; 34:28)
7. After the Israelites built a _ _ _ _ _ _ calf, Moses bowed down before the Lord for forty days and nights. (Deuteronomy 9:16-18)
8. Aaron died forty years after the Israelites left _ _ _ _ _. (Numbers 33:38)
9. Israel was at peace for the last forty years of the life of _ _ _ _ _ _. (Judges 5:31; 8:27)
10. The _ _ _ _ _ _ _ _ _ _ took control of Israel for forty years. (Judges 13:1)
11. Eli was a _ _ _ _ _ in Israel for forty years. (1 Samuel 4:18)
12. _ _ _ _ _ _ _ challenged the Israelite army for forty days before David killed him. (1 Samuel 17:16)
13. The kings _ _ _ _, _ _ _ _ _, _ _ _ _ _ _ _, and _ _ _ _ _ _ _ were reported to have ruled for forty years each. (Acts 13:21; 2 Samuel 5:4; 1 Kings 11:42; 2 Kings 12:1)
14. Solomon had forty thousand stalls of _ _ _ _ _ _ for his chariots. (1 Kings 4:26)
15. Elisha received forty camel loads of gifts from _ _ _ _ _ _ _ _. (2 Kings 8:9)
16. Ezekiel predicted that _ _ _ _ _ would lie in ruins for forty years. (Ezekiel 29:10-11)
17. Jesus _ _ _ _ _ _ for forty days in the wilderness.(Matthew 4:2)
18. After the Resurrection, for a forty-day period, Jesus was revealed to the _ _ _ _ _ _ _ _ _. (Acts 1:3)

ARK BURNING DAMASCUS   DAVID DIED DISCIPLES EGYPT EGYPT
FASTED GIDEON GOLDEN GOLIATH HORSES JEHOASH JUDGE MANNA
MOUNTAIN PHILISTINES RAIN REBEKAH SAUL SOLOMON

```
D E D Y Q Q Y Y D J I L Y D Y D C W F N
I J K M B Q Z A W V X V U H D I H A X S
S S V S A M J O F R M A I S E W O F S P
C X R Q H A G N O F R G R F W D Z Q C H
I S N H S R E B E K A H N E D L O G C L
P N J C E M L J X I E T O I Q G L W T F
L B U U D M D F J F U Y G Y Y U D Y C B
E S F J C M B B T P R H L C L W T R I Q
S N I U B D B C E B Z T S I R Y F R E C
H A U T C P C N W S E A R S P V U Y L R
N G Q D H V K L W V O I V F E E Q V E G
N I A T N U O M G D C L W A C S J K I C
G R P L R H F J U N S O E S G E R D O V
Z B V M T R J Z E B I G O T O M E O F D
M A I B S F K G X L R N W E E O P O H I
P A U E R R A S M G Q K R D N G K X R
X H N I S T P R H L U A S U G D P N W P
M H I N I H O W F P S V W I B I I O V E
A F C L A Y B K G V R O L M Z V O R A V
F E L D I A A T R F X B L T C A A S X P
V N B R L S N G A Q F T O A D Z A P J
O T A M B U T K Q H L P T W M B T E Q S
Y I C R S F B I Z J Y S L H F O H J L J
N H X O B E M K N G E H V F D M N M H G
N Z F L Z Z L F E E H B G Y Y A Z S D N
B Y I T Y O Z S S M S P A O E J A Q R Q
O T R A I P R Q C W N J H E F O U R I Y
Z I E H R J U D G E D B U Y H K G P S S
Z S I C F B R K M Z B Z U E F J O B Q G
T P Y G E R J Y I X N B J G I P B W C X
```

Answers on page 115.

FEELINGS

Read the scriptures below and think about the feelings that Jesus might have had at that time. Remember that Jesus was fully human as well as divine, so you will be thinking about human feelings. You may use some of the feeling words at the bottom of the next page, but do not limit yourself to those words. Use any words you would like to express feelings. There are no wrong answers.

Matthew 21:12-13
When Jesus saw the confusion in the Temple, he might have felt

_____

Matthew 26:6-13
The woman in this story anointed Jesus' head, which was considered an act that might be done for a king. What feelings do you suppose he had for the woman?

_____

How do you think he felt when the disciples spoke against the woman?

_____

Luke 19:28-40
As he rode into Jerusalem on a donkey, Jesus might have felt

_____

Luke 19:41-44
As Jesus looked over Jerusalem, he might have felt

_____

Mark 14:32-42
How might Jesus have felt as he prayed about the events he knew were ahead of him?

_____

When Jesus found his friends asleep instead of praying, how do you suppose he felt?

_____

Luke 22:14-16
What sort of feelings do you suppose Jesus had as they began their meal?

_____

Luke 22:24-34
Look for several feelings that Jesus might have had at this time.

_____

Matthew 26:47-56
Jesus might have had several feelings during this time. What might they have been?

_____

Matthew 26:57-68
What do you suppose were Jesus' feelings as he remained quiet before the priests?

_____

Matthew 27:11-31
How do you suppose Jesus felt as Pilate asked the crowd which person to release?

_____

And how did he feel when the common criminal was released instead of him?

_____

Matthew 27:33-55
How do you suppose Jesus felt:
Toward Simon who carried his cross?

_____

Toward the soldiers who cast lots for his clothes?

_____

Toward the two robbers crucified with him?

_____

When Jesus cried out to God in verse 46?

_____

Matthew 28:1-10
How do you suppose the women felt when they first discovered the empty tomb?

_____

How did they feel when they met Jesus as they ran to tell the disciples?

_____

Words to choose from:

ANGRY, ANXIOUS, CALM, CARING, COMPASSION, CONCERNED, DEJECTED, DELIGHTED, DISAPPOINTED, DISCOURAGED, FRUSTRATED, HAPPY, JILTED, KINDNESS, LET DOWN, LOVING, PEACEFUL, PLEASED, QUIET, REGRETFUL, SAD, SERENE, SHOCKED, SORROWFUL, SORRY, SURPRISED, THANKFUL, TROUBLED, UNHAPPY, UPSET, WORRIED

REPRODUCIBLES

LABYRINTH: A WAY TO MEDITATE

Designs like this were placed on the floors of medieval churches. It is a good tool to help us meditate on God and reflect on our lives. Using your fingers, "walk" this labyrinth in silence. Use the time to pray, to reflect on what's happening in your life, to focus on some question about God, to remember scripture, or simply to quiet yourself. There are no dead ends to a labyrinth. All paths lead to the center and back out again.

EASTERTIDE

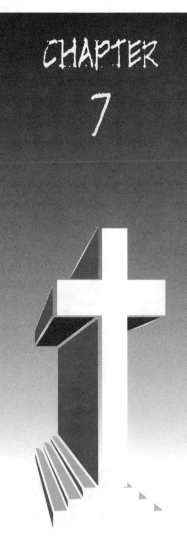

Eastertide is often ignored because we lump Easter Sunday with Holy Week and then move on with our daily lives, forgetting that the Easter season lasts for fifty days until Pentecost. Easter is too important to limit to one day! Perhaps if we develop the habit of using the words Easter Sunday for the day we celebrate Christ's resurrection, we can broaden our thinking to include the season of Easter.

People have always borrowed and adapted symbols and celebrations from surrounding cultures. The Old Testament has many practices that were adaptations of Canaanite preexisting counterparts, such as animal sacrifice, temple worship, circumcision, priests, and prophets. For example, Passover may have been an adaptation from the Canaanite spring festivals. The origin of the word *Easter* is uncertain. It may have come from the Anglo-Saxon goddess of life renewal, Eostre or Eastre, who was celebrated in the spring. Since the resurrection of Christ signifies renewed life, we may have adopted the name and celebration for our purposes.

Many symbols may have also been borrowed and adapted to Christianity. The cross itself is actually an instrument of death that we use as a symbol of new life. The transformation and Christian use of such symbols and celebrations is more important than the origin.

The date of Easter may vary by up to thirty-four days. It is the first Sunday after the full moon crosses the spring equinox, a time set by the Council of Nicea in 325 C.E. This usually places the date between mid March and early April. Early Jewish Christians celebrated it on the third day after Passover, regardless of the day of the week. But as Christianity spread into the Gentile world, it was always celebrated on a Sunday.

Like the season between Christmas and Epiphany, the season between Easter and Pentecost is another time of the year when we allow a lull to develop. It is important to spread the excitement of Easter out over this fifty-day period. Don't let the excitement lag. Keep it active. Use songs and readings of Easter to remind the children of the importance of Christ's resurrection. Greet them with "Happy Easter" during this time and emphasize the change that Christ's resurrection made in the world today.

SIMPLE EXPLANATION

Easter Sunday is the most important day of celebration in our church. It is the day we remember Jesus and how he died instead of compromising his beliefs about God. Although his enemies killed him, God would not let him stay dead. On Easter Sunday, and for fifty days after Easter Sunday, we celebrate the change that God made in the world by raising Jesus from the dead.

SYMBOLS AND COLORS

The symbols and colors for Eastertide are included with the information on Lent found on page 48. The color for Eastertide is white, signifying purity, and is used throughout the fifty days until Pentecost. Gold can also be used during Eastertide to symbolize the kingship of Christ as well as the risen Christ who brings light to a dark world. Many of the symbols are used during Lent as well as Eastertide.

LEARNING ACTIVITIES

RELEASE BUTTERFLIES

Order caterpillars early and watch as they become butterflies. These websites will give you information on when to order and whether or not they are appropriate in your climate: www.insectlore.com and www.butterflywebsite.com. Insect Lore can also be reached by calling 1-800-LIVEBUG. When you release the butterflies, have a special blessing or prayer, thanking God for the symbol of Christ's resurrection and for the new life that Christ brought us.

CREATE BULLETIN BOARDS

These will remind people that we continue to celebrate Christ's resurrection. The children can be instrumental in creating these bulletin boards. Use butterflies and spring flowers, as well as an empty tomb.

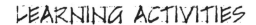

ADD TO THE TIMELINE FROM HOLY WEEK

Add the encounters the disciples had with Jesus using the following scriptures: John 20:19-23; Matthew 28:11-15; John 20:26-31; Luke 24:13-35; Matthew 28:16-20; Luke 24:36-49; John 21:1-25; and Luke 24:50-53. (See page 51 for the timeline.)

COMPARE THE DIFFERENT VERSIONS OF THE STORY

Use the reproducible sheet on pages 70-71 to study the different versions each gospel writer wrote of the Easter story. Remind the children that the writing of the Gospels was done many years after the actual event.

DEVELOP A STROLLING ACTOR

Develop a monologue that tells the Easter story from the viewpoint of a bystander, a soldier, or one of the disciples. This story can have might-have-been additions, such as what the surroundings looked like, what reaction other bystanders might have had, feelings from the actor, and so on. Afterward, explain which part of the story actually comes directly from the Bible and ask how the listeners might have felt if they had been there.

MAKE A LIVE CROSS

Wrap a wooden cross with chicken wire and invite children to bring flowers from their yards to create a live flower cross. If garden flowers are not available, contact a local florist about using leftover flowers from the past few days. They will usually give them to you at no charge. The children may sponsor this project and invite the whole church to participate.

FILL A ROOM WITH FLOWERS

As they arrive, give each child a small garden plant that is blooming (such as a petunia or pansy) and ask them to take it to their room and use the plants to form a cross. Then they will take their part of the cross home and plant it in their yard to remember the Eastertide celebration. This need not be reserved for Easter Sunday but is appropriate for another Sunday in Eastertide, reminding the children that we continue to celebrate Easter even after Easter Sunday.

EXPLORE EGG TRADITIONS

The egg has been a tradition of Easter for many years. The egg reminds us of the tomb where Jesus was placed after his death. The fact that the baby chick breaks out of the egg reminds us of Jesus coming out of the closed tomb at his resurrection. Consider these egg traditions from around the world.

Jewish tradition—the egg is a part of the Passover Seder meal, representing hope and a new life after escaping from slavery.

Chinese tradition—a red egg is sent to friends when a baby is one month old. This is an invitation to a celebration feast for the child's birth.

Scottish tradition—an egg is placed beneath the seeds that are sown in the fields in the spring to symbolize a good harvest and new life from the seed.

Ukrainian tradition—giving a decorated egg symbolizes giving a gift of love to that person.

German tradition—when you break the shell of an Easter egg, you allow the blessing of Easter to enter your home.

DO A CROSSWORD PUZZLE

To review Lent and Holy Week and also to recognize symbols and colors of Easter, use the reproducible "Colors and Symbols for Lent and Easter" on page 58.

WORSHIP SUGGESTIONS

USE VISUAL IMAGERY

On Easter Sunday, you can create an image of a cave by stacking several rocks to form the "cave" with one rock as the closure. Inside the cave place a lighted candle to represent Christ coming out of the tomb. Other visuals might include butterflies, spring bulb flowers, bare branches and budded branches, and other signs of new life at spring.

BRING IN LIGHT

Begin your worship by asking everyone to wait outside. When all have assembled, give each person a candle and light it as they enter the room, which you have darkened. Each light brings more brightness to the room, symbolizing the new light that Christ brought to a dark world.

USE BAPTISM VOWS

Consider using the vows from your baptism service, remembering how we are renewed by Christ.

SING TOGETHER

Use hymns such as those listed below and remind the children that we celebrate a living Christ.

"Christ Is Risen"
"Christ the Lord Is Risen Today"
"He Is Lord"
"He Lives"
"Up from the Grave He Arose"

EACH PERSON'S STORY

The disciples expected Jesus to return to earth in a short time, therefore they didn't actually write down the happenings of that first Easter morning until many years later. Each one remembered a different part of the story, so we have several versions. Use your Bible and the chart below to see how each story differs.

MATTHEW 28:1-10	MARK 16:1-11	LUKE 24:1-43	JOHN 20, 21
Mary Magdalene and other Mary	Mary Magdalene and Mary (mother of James), and Salome bought spices	The women (Mary Magdalene, Joanna, Mary the mother of James, and others) carry spices	Mary Magdalene
	"Who will roll stone?"		
Violent earthquake			
Angel rolled back the stone and sat on it			
Guards afraid			
	Women see stone already moved and enter tomb.	Found stone rolled away. Went in and were puzzled.	Found stone rolled away.
Angel to women: Do not be afraid. He is not here. He has been raised. Come, see the place. Go and tell disciples. He is going ahead to Galilee.	Young man in white, sitting at right: Do not be alarmed. He is risen. Look where he was placed. Go and tell disciples and Peter. He goes ahead to Galilee	Two men, bright and shining, said: Why look among the dead? He is alive. He is not here. He is raised.	
Women ran to tell disciples.			
Jesus greeted them. They worship him. Jesus said to tell followers to go to Galilee.			
	They ran terrified and said nothing to anyone. (Another old ending says they told Peter and his friends.)	Women returned and told all. Peter was the only one who believed.	She ran and told Simon Peter and the disciple whom Jesus loved: They have taken him. We don't know where they put him.
		Peter ran to the tomb. Bent down and saw cloths. Went home amazed.	Peter and the other disciple ran to tomb. Other disciple ran faster, looked in but did not go in. Peter went straight in. Then the other disciple went in.

REPRODUCIBLES

MATTHEW 28:1-10	MARK 16:1-11	LUKE 24:1-43	JOHN 20, 21
Guards report to chief priests.			
	Second ending: Jesus appeared to Mary Magdalene.		
			Mary cried outside the tomb. She saw two angels: "Woman, why are you weeping?" Mary: "They have taken away my Lord." She turned and saw Jesus but did not recognize him.
			Jesus said, "Woman, why are you weeping? Whom are you looking for?" Mary thought he was the gardener: "If you took him, I will go and get him." Jesus: "Mary!" Mary: "Rabbouni!" Jesus: Do not hold on to me but go and tell others.
	She told others, but they did not believe.		Mary told the disciples.
	Jesus appeared "in a different manner" to two of them while they were on their way to the country. They returned and told the others, who still did not believe.	Jesus meets followers on road to Emmaus.	
	Jesus appeared to the eleven as they were eating.	After those from Emmaus tell disciples, Jesus appears to them, showing them his hands and feet. He ate fish with them.	Late Sunday, the disciples were behind locked doors. Jesus came, showing his hands and feet. Thomas wasn't there, but Jesus later appears to him.
			Jesus later appears to the disciples at the lake while they fish.

PENTECOST

We often consider Pentecost as the birthday of the church, and for young children, this is the best explanation. Without the Holy Spirit that came at Pentecost, there would not be a church, because it was the Holy Spirit that ignited the flame of evangelism that spread the message throughout the world.

In the subtropical country of Israel, there was an early harvest, and the Hebrew celebration of Pentecost marked that harvest. The celebration took place on the fiftieth day after Passover and had several names: Festival of the Fifty Days, Day of Firstfruits, Festival of Weeks, and Shabuoth. Old Testament reference to this festival is found in Leviticus 23:15-16. During Jesus' lifetime, the festival was no longer associated with harvest but had become a day to celebrate the giving of the Torah (the Law) on Mount Sinai.

At this festival, fifty days after the Resurrection, people converged on Jerusalem from all directions, filling the city with various cultures and languages. In the midst of this chaos, the Holy Spirit came to those early disciples who did not know what to do next. The Spirit united them in purpose and in language, allowing them to understand each other and focus on their mission.

For many years, Pentecost became the accepted time for new converts to join the church. New members wore white robes when they were baptized. Therefore, Pentecost became known as White Sunday. We take our name for the day from the word the Greeks used: *pentekoste hemera*, meaning "fiftieth day."

The day for Pentecost changes just as Easter Sunday changes, depending on the moon cycle. It can occur any time between May 10 and June 13. Some churches celebrate Pentecost for only one day, while others celebrate and use the color red for several weeks before moving to the Ordinary Season or Kingdomtide.

No matter how long your church celebrates, be sure that it is a joyful celebration! As the birthday of the church, we can celebrate in a festive mood. Just as the first disciples were "drunk" with the Holy Spirit, we can be overcome with joy in Christ.

SIMPLE EXPLANATION

Pentecost is the day that the Holy Spirit came to direct the disciples. We consider it the birthday of the church because this is the time when the followers of Jesus united and became so excited; the message of Christ then spread like wildfire. We might say that this was the day that they "caught on fire" for Christ. The scripture uses the image of flames to explain their excitement.

SYMBOLS AND COLORS

Color:	red	flame of Holy Spirit
Symbols:	boat	Church
	curled lines	Rush of wind—Holy Spirit
	dove	Holy Spirit
	flame	Holy Spirit
	rainbow	Holy Spirit

LEARNING ACTIVITIES

CREATE AND USE A LITANY

Using the reproducible sheet on page 11, create a Pentecost litany. The story of Pentecost is found in Acts 1:8 and 2:1-21. You may also find the following scripture passages that speak of fire, light, and the Spirit helpful: Exodus 13:21; Isaiah 60:19; Matthew 5:14-16; Luke 12:49; John 3:6; and Hebrews 12:28-29.

BAKE BREADS

Baking various ethnic breads can help children recognize the multicultural community that was a part of the first Pentecost. If you bake several breads, make arrangements for these breads to be used by the congregation for communion. See pages 94-96 for some recipes.

CREATE WIND ITEMS

Create items that pertain to the wind as you talk about the wind of the Holy Spirit engulfing the followers at Pentecost. These might include wind chimes, wind socks, kites, and pinwheels. Use symbols of the season to decorate the items.

WRITE NEWS REPORTS

Choose radio call letters and write a news report on any or all of the subjects below. Or write the report as newspaper article(s). Have the children choose biblical names to use for themselves as reporters. Review the life of Jesus for this, plus Acts 2:1-15, 42-47.

- Death of Jesus with review of miracles he performed
- Resurrection
- Disciples dejected and in hiding
- Pentecost experience—"Can you believe this?"
- Followers banded together—sold their possessions

USE RED EVERYWHERE

Use red in any way possible, talking about how red represents the flame of the Holy Spirit that was given at Pentecost.

- Encourage everyone to wear red.
- Plant red flowers around the church.
- Distribute red flowers or red ribbons.
- Use red balloons, candles, streamers, banners, food items, and so on.

MAKE RED CANDLES

As you do this ask the children how fire reminds them of God's presence with us. (Some examples would be: Fire takes away the darkness and gives us light. The color and movement of fire can be joyful. Fire gives us warmth and in cold weather keeps us alive. Fire can burn away impurities.)

You will need the following to make the candle:

8 oz. or 10 oz. cans or jars
wax (use paraffin or old candles)
red crayons
double boiler and stove
wick
construction paper or markers

- Put the wax and crayons in the top of the double boiler with water in the bottom.
- Melt the wax over low heat.
- Pour the wax into the cans or jars. (If you use jars, be sure they are hot so that they don't crack.)
- Dip pieces of wick (longer than the cans or jars) into the hot wax and immediately put under running cold water, keeping the wick straight.

- When the wax in the cans or jars is partially cool but still soft, poke a hole in the middle and insert the stiff wick.
- Pour additional liquid wax around the wick to fill the hole.
- Decorate the candle with bright construction paper or markers.

BURN THE PAST

The flame of the Holy Spirit at Pentecost helps us realize that Christ brings a new future. Ask children to write their mistakes, rejections, disappointments, and worries on pieces of paper. Then have a time when you burn these, reminding them that God's love burns the past, and we start anew. In starting new, we will try to follow God's guidance in everything we do.

EXPLORE THE USE OF FIRE

Enjoy popping corn and then talk together about how fire/heat made a difference in the popcorn. The "life" of the popcorn changed because of the fire/heat. Discuss how we use fire in positive ways. How can God make a difference in our lives as the heat made a difference in popcorn? Remind them that at Pentecost the disciples were "ignited" with their faith as if they were on fire. (A fun way to do this is to use an electric corn popper and place it on a clean sheet on the floor. Leave the lid off as it heats and the corn will pop out of the popper and onto the clean sheet. Sit around the sheet and eat the corn as it pops.)

USE A PRAYER WEB

This can be used to help children express thanks for what they like about the church.

Stand or sit in a circle for this prayer. You may choose to sit on the floor. As you begin, hold on to the end of a ball of string or yarn (or wrap it around your finger) and mention something that you would like to thank God for or to pray about. Then ask if there is someone else who has something to add. Roll the string ball (or you may throw the ball) to that person, making a string connection between you and that person. After sharing, that person will hold on to the string and roll the ball to another. As you proceed across the circle, you will create a web with the string. If you are rolling the ball, everyone will need to hold the string high during the rolling; if throwing the ball, hold the string next to the floor.

After all who want to speak have shared, ask those who did not share to take hold of the string so that everyone is connected to the web. Close the experience with a simple sentence, "God, we ask you to hear all that we have talked about along our prayer web. Amen."[1]

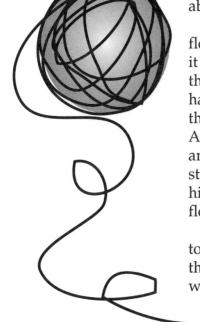

CLIMB A PENTECOST LADDER

As a group, retell the story of Pentecost. Pass out copies of the Pentecost Ladder from the reproducible sheet on page 80. Have students take turns reading each "step," beginning at the bottom. Then ask the class to repeat Step 12 in unison and with enthusiasm! Lead a brief discussion about how the students can share Christ with others in the coming week. If appropriate, tell them they will have an opportunity to share their experiences during the next class or meeting.

USE GUIDED MEDITATION

Ask the children to sit comfortably with their feet on the floor and their hands in their laps and eyes closed. Lead them in this guided meditation. If you have a recording of wind blowing, use it in the background.

After the meditation, ask if anyone would like to share any feelings they had during the experience. Don't force anyone to talk, but be open to those who want to share.

> Imagine that you are in a room with friends. You are very sad because someone you love has died—someone who was a great influence on you; someone who helped you know just what you should do. You're not sure just where you should go or what you should do now. (pause)
>
> Suddenly you hear the sound of a mighty wind filling the room! It swirls around you, touching you on all sides, as if it surrounds you and swallows you up. (pause) You look around, and it appears that tiny flames of fire are on everyone's heads. The flames do not burn, but they brighten the whole room! The flames are reflected in the eyes of all your friends in the room, and you see excitement there! (pause)
>
> Now you hear voices coming from all areas of the room, and you realize that everyone is speaking in a different language. This puzzles you because just before this you all had difficulty talking with people from other countries who were visiting your city. You start to talk and realize that you can also speak in a language you couldn't use before. You wonder what this means. (pause)
>
> Now, everything is quiet, and the wind and the flames are gone. But there is, instead, a feeling of the presence of God. Could this be the Holy Spirit that your friend promised would come after his death? (pause)
>
> When you are ready, open your eyes.

USE DIFFERENT LANGUAGE GREETINGS

Here are a few translations for "Welcome" that you can learn and teach to the children. Concentrate on a different one each week of the season.

Spanish	Bienvenido
French	Bienvenue
German	Willkommen
Italian	Benvenuto
Portuguese	Boa vinda
Norwegian	Mottakelse
Dutch	Welkom

DEMONSTRATE SEVERAL LANGUAGES

Secure a recording of another language or have someone record a common scripture in another language. Play this for the children and ask them if they understand what is being said. You might even have several tape recorders playing several languages at once and ask if they can understand any of it. Then read Acts 2:1-12 and talk about how the Holy Spirit helped everyone understand one another.

WORSHIP SUGGESTIONS

USE VISUAL IMAGERY

Use anything that symbolizes wind or fire, such as kites, balloons, flames, red streamers, and even red peppers. You could also use rocks, indicating the solid foundation of the church, or a birthday cake.

USE GUIDED MEDITATION (SEE P. 77)

USE GUIDED MEDITATION (SEE P. 77)

LIGHT CANDLES

As you close, stand in a circle and give everyone a candle. Light the candle of each person individually, saying "(Name), you are God's light to lighten the world."

SING TOGETHER

Use hymns like those listed below and remind the children that we celebrate the church at Pentecost.

"Bind Us Together, Lord"
"Breathe on Me, Breath of God"
"Every Time I Feel the Spirit"
"I'm Goin'a Sing When the Spirit Says Sing"
"Pass It On"
"Spirit of the Living God"
"Surely the Presence of the Lord"
"Sweet, Sweet Spirit"
"We Are the Church"

PENTECOST LADDER

12. I go out, ready to share Christ with others!

11. I know what I must do now! I must tell others about Jesus and how he taught me to rely on God.

10. Everything becomes quiet. What could this mean?

9. I realize that I can speak to the people who have come to the city from different countries.

8. Everyone is speaking languages they could never speak before.

7. There is a light of excitement in their eyes.

6. I look around, and all of my friends seem to have tongues of flame on their heads.

5. I wonder where it came from.

4. Suddenly there is a rush of wind, as if the heavens opened up!

3. I meet with my friends in a special room.

2. There are many people in town who speak many different languages. I feel very alone.

1. I miss my friend, Jesus, who helped me in many ways.

SEASON AFTER PENTECOST (KINGDOMTIDE)

CHAPTER 9

The season after Pentecost is the longest block of time of any season. It lasts until the beginning of Advent. Some churches will continue to celebrate Pentecost for several weeks, and some move directly to this season. This season is also called *Kingdomtide.* This is one of the ordinary seasons. The word *ordinary*, in this case, has no reference to "common" or "mundane." This comes from the word *ordinal*, which simply means "counted" or "chronological time." This is time in order.

During this season, after the fire and excitement of Pentecost, it is natural to look at the way the message of Christ has spread, and continues to be spread, throughout the world. This is a good time to look at God's people everywhere and what we can do in mission with them. Ministry to persons outside our comfort zone is often ignored, except for an occasional gift of money. This is a time when we can involve children in hands-on ministry to others. This is a time to help them get out into the world beyond their immediate circle of friends.

This season offers a great opportunity to recognize the difference between multicultural education, which emphasizes our differences, and global awareness, which sees other cultures as related to ours and stresses similarities. Avoid the "foreign" image of other countries. Even in their dress, most countries have more similarities than differences.

Our study of stewardship also happens during this season, linking stewardship of our time, talents, and money with the mission that we see God leading us into. Stewardship and mission are like the head and feet of ministry. Stewardship tells us what, how, and why we are in ministry, and mission actually puts action to that ministry. Middle and older elementary children can understand that God calls them to be in ministry to others, and younger elementary children can be challenged to think of ways that they can help another person.

SIMPLE EXPLANATION

After the disciples' experience at Pentecost, they began spreading the news about Jesus to other countries. The season after Pentecost, or *Kingdomtide*, is a time when we think about all that God has given us and how we can help spread the news to others.

SYMBOLS AND COLORS

Colors:	green	growth
Symbols:	leaves/plants	Growth of church
	cross above globe	Christ's message to all the world

LEARNING ACTIVITIES

LEARN/ILLUSTRATE PRAYER

The Prayer of Saint Francis of Assisi is a good guide for sharing God's love with others. Look at the words and how they apply to our lives today. Use the reproducible sheet on page 86 to learn the words. The children can fill in the empty frames as they think about their own lives.

DISCUSS HOW THE BIBLE MESSAGE SPREAD

Use the reproducible on pages 88-89 to talk about how the Bible message was passed along through the years. The children may use pencils to follow the path of the message as you talk about it.

FOLLOW CHURCH MISSION PROJECTS

Post a world map on the wall or bulletin board with pictures or stories about mission projects that your church participates in, both physically and monetarily, in your country and other countries. Don't forget to include projects supported by your national church organization.

Nearby post a picture of your church. Use different brightly colored yarns to connect your church to the mission project and then to the spot on the map where the mission takes place.

RESEARCH CHURCH STEWARDSHIP

Assign groups to research how your church uses the money that the congregation contributes. Assign the groups to interview the following (and any other appropriate individuals): office staff, trustees, people who work with education (all age levels), missions, worship, music, personnel committee, and so on. Be sure that the following information is requested: salaries, cleaning supplies and equipment, office supplies and equipment, phone, water, electricity, lawn care, vans, gas for trips, music and instruments, toys, curriculum, Bibles, library books, and hymnals.

Create a mural or another way to illustrate what they learned. Talk about how we reach out to others in the community and around the world when we support our church.

LIST TREASURED POSSESSIONS

This activity will help children think about how important material possessions actually are. Ask each child to list five of their most treasured possessions. Then ask these questions:

- What might you have done with the money you spent on some of your possessions if you had not bought them?
- What would you do with the time you spend with those possessions if you did not have them?
- Think about each possession individually.
- Think of the first possession on your list. Does this cause you *not* to follow Christ to your best ability? (Pause)
- Think of the second (third, fourth, fifth) on your list. Does this cause you *not* to follow Christ to your best ability? (Pause)

You might follow these questions by asking each child to make a written commitment to use one possession differently in the future.

Example: Some children may spend all their money on music, DVDs, or special clothes and give none to special projects for the church. Or they may spend all their time looking at videos and have no time to help someone who needs them.[1]

LEARN ABOUT WATER

Water is an element that we can't live without, but it is scarce in many areas of the world. Learning to care for others involves knowing about how they live. Use the reproducible on page 87 to discuss water. Then have a water jug relay.

"Fill 10 one-gallon jugs with water. Divide into two teams, and give each team 5 jugs. Explain that in Kenya, 5 gallons a day is the amount of water each family uses. Remind them that this does not

include water for lengthy showers, dishwashers, washing cars, or other uses.

"Run a relay race, each person carrying all 5 jugs from one point to another. " (Let each child decide whether to try to carry several gallons at once or make several trips.) "The winning team gets the privilege of using some of the water to make lemonade and serve everyone. Be sure that all leftover water is not wasted, but used in some way."[2]

WRITE A CINQUAIN (SIN-CANE) POEM

Poetry helps children express their thoughts. It gives structure to creative thinking. You might have a thesaurus available to help the children think of words. Use this formula to write the poem, but first ask them to brainstorm some of the words that you might use on each line before you decide on exact words. For a poem about missions you might use water, hunger, helping, caring, or a specific country you've studied. For a subject around stewardship you might use talents, money, time, fresh air, creation, or earth.

Line 1: One-word title or subject.
Line 2: Two words that tell about the subject. These words compose a phrase, or they may be separate words.
Line 3: Three verbs or action words (such as "ing" words), or a three-word phrase about the subject.
Line 4: Four words that tell about the writer's feelings on the subject.
Line 5: The subject word again, or another word that refers back to the title or subject. If the poem is a prayer, this word may be "Amen."

Example:

Hunger
no food
pain dizziness stumbling
I cannot even think.
Help![3]

RESEARCH NEWSPAPERS

Provide newspapers for the children to search through and locate stories of people who have acted toward others in caring ways.

WORSHIP SUGGESTIONS

CREATE AND USE A LITANY

Use the Prayer of Saint Francis of Assisi on page 86 to create a litany. Decide who, or what group, will read which lines and then use it during worship.

SING TOGETHER

Use hymns such as those listed below and remind the children that we celebrate our opportunity to spread God's Word to others.

"Arise, Shine Out, Your Light Has Come"
"Christ for the World We Sing"
"Here I Am, Lord"
"I Love to Tell the Story"
"Pass It On"
"The Voice of God Is Calling"
"We Are Marching in the Light of God"
"We've a Story to Tell to the Nations"

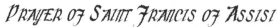

PRAYER OF SAINT FRANCIS OF ASSISI

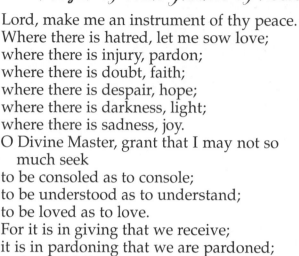

Lord, make me an instrument of thy peace.
Where there is hatred, let me sow love;
where there is injury, pardon;
where there is doubt, faith;
where there is despair, hope;
where there is darkness, light;
where there is sadness, joy.
O Divine Master, grant that I may not so
    much seek
to be consoled as to console;
to be understood as to understand;
to be loved as to love.
For it is in giving that we receive;
it is in pardoning that we are pardoned;
and it is in dying that we are born
    to eternal life.
Amen.

What can I do to make someone hopeful?

What can I give to others?

What can I do to brighten someone's day?

Who has wronged me that I can tell "I forgive you"?

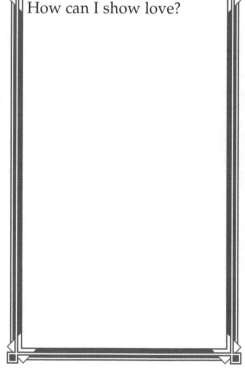

How can I show love?

How can I listen better to someone else?

WATER FACTS

No life on earth is possible without water.

Water provides a home for nearly 90% of all living plants.

Water covers 75% of the earth's surface, but 99% of the water is either salt water in the oceans or frozen in glaciers.

If all the glacier ice that exists today melted, a layer of water approximately 196 feet deep would be added to the world's oceans—and many coastal lands would be submerged.

You can live without food for more than a month, but without water for less than a week.

Every day 1 billion people on earth drink contaminated water.

25,000 people die every day for lack of clean drinking water.

About 80% of all sickness and disease can be attributed to inadequate water or sanitation.

Although only a fifth of a gallon is all one needs to survive, a person must take in 2½ quarts of water a day to maintain a normal water balance in the body.

Mothers in some countries walk 15 miles each day for water, sometimes requiring 8 hours a day. In the U.S., on the average, we use 200 gallons of water a day per person.

It takes water to make things:

One Sunday newspaper takes about 150 gallons

One automobile tire takes about 2,000 gallons

One slice of bread takes about 37 gallons

One ton of oil takes about 180 tons of water

One ton of paper takes about 250 tons of water

One ton of grain takes about 1,000 tons of water

REPRODUCIBLES

Oral Tradition—the stories were told in family groups and in the community, often around campfires.

Later people began to use pictures to represent certain words. Now they could tell the stories without having to be there. Sometimes these pictures were put on soft clay or wax tablets, or they were scratched into the walls of caves. They were also carved into stone.

About the same time, they learned to prepare animal skins so well that they could be written on. Very thin, tanned leather was called parchment.

To make the leather or parchment pieces easier to handle, they were sewn together and made into scrolls.

"About 3000 B.C. the people in Egypt learned how to make something like paper called papyrus" by placing papyrus reeds together and mashing them. The words were written on papyrus scrolls, but this was very expensive, so they did not waste papyrus with details that the people already knew.

In 1436 the printing press was invented. Now copies that looked identical could be made in a shorter time.

Many people believed that the Bible should be read only by the priests, and many of the early printed Bibles were burned.

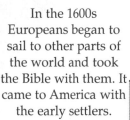

About 1500, more people lived in cities, and schools were started. Then more people could read.

In the 1600s Europeans began to sail to other parts of the world and took the Bible with them. It came to America with the early settlers.

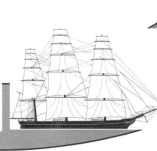

In the 1800s, Bible societies were formed to translate the Bible into languages for missionaries to use in their work.

BYBEL
Bibbia Bíblia
Bibel
Biblia

About 1700 B.C. we began to make up letters to represent certain sounds, and the stories were written down.

"Around 100 A.D. the Romans got the idea of sewing sheets [of parchment] together at the middle and folding them, like the books we have today. These early books were called 'codex' books." They were easier to store and to find your place when reading.

Because most people did not know how to read, they usually learned the Bible in a singsong method of repeating what the scribes or teachers told them.

The actual words of the Bible were copied by hand from one codex book to another, usually by monks who dedicated their lives to this. The Old Testament books had been copied from one scroll to another by persons called scribes.

As the Bible spread from one country to another, people had to translate the message from one language to another. The words did not always mean the same thing, and so different translators interpreted the words differently.

Many people thought the Bible should only be read in Latin, but in about 1380 John Wycliffe translated it into English.

The pages of the Bible were sometimes decorated with drawings in color. These were called "illuminated" Bibles.

Earlier (about 200 B.C.), the Chinese had invented paper. "Some Chinese prisoners were taken to Arabia around 900 A.D., where they taught the Arabs. The Arabs taught the Moors, who lived in northern Africa. The Moors conquered Spain. While they were in Spain they made paper, the first time it was made in Europe, around 1250 A.D."

With the invention of records, tapes, and videos, recordings of the Bible were made.

The computer made the Bible very compact and easy to search. The Internet connects the Bible to people all around the world.

And so we have the Bible in many forms today! You can read it anywhere you like.

REPRODUCIBLES

OTHER SPECIAL DAYS

Trinity Sunday

The Sunday after Pentecost is celebrated as Trinity Sunday, but too often gets lost in the shuffle. This is the Sunday when we recognize that God comes to us in three ways: as a parent (Father), in human form (Son), and within us (Holy Spirit). It is too easy to concentrate on these individually and not see them as reflections of one God. Because we are all different in the ways that we grow spiritually, we may relate to one facet of God more than another.

Young children, who are concrete thinkers, cannot understand the abstract concept of the Trinity. As they grow older and their ability to think abstractly matures, they can begin to see how we experience God in many ways and that our labeling these three ways of experiencing God can be referred to as the Trinity. However, no matter how young children may be, we can help them have experiences of these three facets of God that they will label later.

SIMPLE EXPLANATION

On Trinity Sunday we explore three ways that we understand God. God can be like a parent (Father), a human being (Son/Jesus), and within us (Holy Spirit). We call these three ways of understanding God the Trinity.

LEARNING ACTIVITIES

THINK ABOUT ROLES

Divide the children into five groups and assign each group one of the five sections at the top of the reproducible on page 107. Ask them to follow the directions on the page. They can discuss it in their groups, but then have each person fill in the frames with his or her own answers. Ask them to wait to answer the questions at the bottom.

Give the following as an example:

Your brother might be: brother, cousin, grandson, son, nephew, student, musician, quarterback, and so on.

CHAPTER 10

After they have had time to make their lists, look at the questions at the bottom of the page and discuss them as a class. Then tell them that we often see God as several roles.

- We know God to be like a parent, like the best parent we could ever know—not one who just gives us lots of gifts, but one who loves us more than anything else in the world.
- We know God as Jesus who came to earth to show us what God was like and so that we realize that God had a human experience too.
- We know God who works within us, as the Holy Spirit.
- We call these three ways of understanding God "the Trinity." On Trinity Sunday we celebrate those three ways of knowing God.

FIND HIDDEN PICTURES

Ask the children to look at the reproducible "Three in One" on page 108. Ask them to see if they can find at least 20 objects with three parts in the picture, such as a triangle.

STUDY CREEDS

Explain that a creed is a statement of what we believe. Creeds have been used in the church for hundreds of years. Review several of the historic creeds and compare the way each phrases the belief in the Trinity. Ask the children what they would put in a creed if they were to write one. Invite them to write their own creeds.

MAKE A GRAFFITI WALL

At the top of a long paper write the phrase, "God is like. . . ." Ask the children to draw and write statements of what God is like. Explain that when we speak of the Trinity, we are saying that we understand God in three different ways.

CREATE A BULLETIN COVER

Ask the children to draw symbols of the Trinity that can be used on a bulletin cover. These may include triangles, trefoil, three intertwined circles, fleurs-de-lis, or a shamrock. Flowers with three parts, such as the iris, may also be used.

WORSHIP SUGGESTIONS

USE A CREED

Use one of the historic creeds in worship. If you created a creed, you may use that also.

PRAY IN TRIADS

Ask the children to stand in threes as you pray. Use a prayer similar to this: "Thank you God for the many ways that we come to know you. We thank you for loving us like a wonderful parent. We thank you for understanding what it is like to be human. We thank you for helping us through our hard times. Amen."

SING TOGETHER

Use hymns such as those listed below as a way of reminding the children that we celebrate the many ways that we can experience God.

"Come, Thou Almighty King"
"God Hath Spoken by the Prophets"
"God of Many Names"
"God of the Sparrow God of the Whale"
"How Like a Gentle Spirit"
"On Eagle's Wings"
"Our Parent, by Whose Name"

Worldwide Communion Day

This special day, the first Sunday in October, is recent in history. It gives Christians worldwide the opportunity to receive communion on the same date, uniting across national boundaries and denominations. It is a time to recognize our common love for Christ and to learn of others who serve in Christ's mission.

This is an ideal time to stress the unity we have as Christians. Although we may be divided in many ways, we are united in Christ. Middle and older elementary children have enough background in geography to really appreciate this unity overcoming our diversity. Use this day to stress the importance of Christians striving to make a better world, no matter where we are.

SIMPLE EXPLANATION

On the first Sunday in October, each year, Christians around the world take part in a communion service. By doing this on one special day we realize that Christians worldwide love Christ, no matter where we live or what language we speak.

LEARNING ACTIVITIES

BAKE BREADS

Use several ethnic recipes to bake bread that can be used for communion or a love feast. As you work with the various breads, talk about some of the culture and customs of the people and how God created each of us different, yet alike. Here are some recipes you might try, or use your own.

SWEET BREAD FROM INDIA

2 cups plain flour
¼ teaspoon salt
⅔ cup water
¼ cup sugar
1 tablespoon vegetable oil
Stove top griddle or electric fry pan

- Stir flour, salt, and water together until it makes a large ball.
- Knead the dough for a short time on a lightly floured surface.
- Divide the dough into 2-inch balls and cover the pieces with a damp cloth or plastic wrap.
- Roll and cook each dough ball, one at a time in the following method:

- roll the dough ball out very thin
- sprinkle lightly and evenly with sugar
- fold up dough into a small square and roll out again until thin
- lightly oil a griddle and heat over medium heat (or use an electric fry pan)
- cook until golden brown, 30 seconds to 1 minute on each side
Serve immediately.

NORWEGIAN OR SWEDISH LEFSA (POTATO FLAT BREAD)

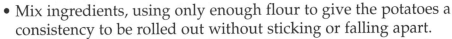

3 cups cooled mashed potatoes
3 cups flour (or less, depending on moistness of potatoes)
1 teaspoon salt
1 tablespoon sugar
2 tablespoons shortening
2 tablespoons cream
pastry cloth or floured surface
stove top griddle or electric fry pan

- Mix ingredients, using only enough flour to give the potatoes a consistency to be rolled out without sticking or falling apart.
- Roll out on floured pastry cloth, as if for pie crust, using only enough additional flour to keep from sticking. Roll as thin as possible. (Using sleeve on rolling pin also helps.)
- Bake on hot griddle (400°) on both sides. An electric fry pan is good for this. Do not overcook.
- Cool on dishtowel and fold into squares.
- To eat, unfold and spread with soft butter and a sugar cinnamon mix. Roll up and enjoy!

CUBAN BREAD

6 ½ cups unsifted flour
2 packages dry yeast
2 cups water
2 tablespoons sugar
2 teaspoons salt
Yellow cornmeal

- Stir together 2 cups of the flour and the yeast in the large bowl of an electric mixer.
- Heat water, sugar and salt, until very warm to the touch (not hot), stirring constantly.
- Add to the flour-yeast blend.
- Beat about 3 minutes at high speed or until smooth.
- Stir in enough additional flour to make stiff dough; turn out on lightly floured surface. Knead 12 to 15 minutes or until the dough becomes bouncy and elastic.

- Cover with a large bowl and let rest 45 minutes.
- Grease a baking sheet and sprinkle lightly with the cornmeal.
- Divide dough into thirds.
- Using a rolling pin, roll each third into a rectangle about 13 by 10 inches. Starting from the widest side, roll each rectangle jelly-roll fashion, pressing the dough into the roll at each turn; press ends together to seal and fold ends slightly under the loaf.
- Place seam side down on baking sheet. Make small diagonal cuts across the top of each loaf with a sharp knife. Brush all over with water. Let rise in a warm place until doubled, about 20 minutes.
- Place loaves in a cold oven and bake 45-50 minutes at 400°.

Cover lightly with foil if they brown too rapidly.

Cool on racks before cutting. Makes 3 loaves.

TEACH PEACE IN SEVERAL LANGUAGES

Teach the children to say "Peace be with you" in several languages.

Dutch	De vrede zijnd met u.
French	La paix soit avec vous.
German	Frieden ist mit Ihnen.
Italian	La pace è con voi.
Norwegian	Fred er med De.
Portuguese	A paz seja com você.
Spanish	La paz esté con usted.

LEARN ABOUT A COUNTRY

Each year select a different country where your church is in mission. Learn about the people, their customs in celebrating communion, and how Christianity is influencing that country. Bake a bread typical of that country. If the bread can be used in an all-church service for communion, arrange for the children to present the bread at the time it is consecrated for communion and for information about the country to be placed in the bulletin.

WRITE LETTERS

Contact your church mission agency for addresses and write to missionaries in different countries, asking about their traditions in their church. The children can share some of the things that they like about their own church in their letters.

WORSHIP SUGGESTIONS

USE VISUAL IMAGERY

Use a globe or world map, objects from several cultures, or a dove symbolizing peace as visual imagery on a worship or celebration table. If communion is served, the single loaf and one cup signifies all one body in Christ.

LA PAZ ESTÉ CON USTED.

La pace è con voi.

la paix soit avec vous,

FRIEDEN IST MIT IHNEN

SING TOGETHER

Use hymns like those listed below and remind the children that we celebrate the family of Christ that reaches around the world.

"Bind Us Together, Lord"
"Blest Be the Tie That Binds"
"Christ for the World We Sing"
"For the Healing of the Nations"
"God of Grace and God of Glory"
"Help Us Accept Each Other"
"In Christ There Is No East or West"
"Let There Be Light"
"Let There Be Peace on Earth"
"Let Us Break Bread Together"
"Lift Every Voice and Sing"
"O God of Every Nation"
"One Bread, One Body"
"Shalom to You"
"They'll Know We Are Christians by Our Love"
"This Is My Song"
"We, Thy People, Praise Thee"

Halloween / All Saints' Day

Before Christ, the Celts celebrated the end of the summer and prepared for the coming of the dark months the only way they knew how. This celebration was on October 31. Since their religion believed that evil spirits hovered over the earth, ready to pounce on them in the dark, they burned fires and made animal sacrifices to keep the evil spirits away. They did not have the scientific knowledge that we have today, so they believed that witches had magical powers. The word *witch* comes from the Old-English word *wicce*, or "wise one," and it was originally thought that witches possessed magic that was good and evil. Witches were believed to cause storms, diseases, and deaths. A woman could be declared a witch simply because she had a birthmark or because she was able to float in water. Anything that people could not understand was blamed on evil spirits and witches. Instead of relying on superstition, we now understand many scientific laws of our world and can predict natural disasters. We know that many diseases come from germs and lack of sanitation. We can warn people who are likely to have heart attacks, and our scientists are working to discover causes for cancer and other fatal illnesses.

While the Celts were practicing their religion, Christianity was growing in the Roman Empire. As Christianity began to span over generations, there were more and more people who had died for their beliefs and who were remembered in special ways. The Roman Catholic Church established special days to remember specific persons, designating them as "saints." When it became evident that there were more saints than days to celebrate, the church established a specific day to commemorate all those who did not have a special day set aside for them.

In the ninth century, to combat the old Celtic religion in the British Isles, the church proclaimed November 1 as All Saints' Day and the night of October 31 as All Hallows' Eve, or Halloween. Christianity focused on the brighter side of these holidays, switching the emphasis from evil to the worship of the true God. This illustrates the difference that Christianity made in the world.

We now recognize each person who loves the Lord as a "saint," whether living or dead, and so All Saints' Day is now broader than the celebration of those who have died. We see this time as an occasion to remember our heritage and those who have gone before us and also an opportunity to recognize our responsibility to carry Christianity forward as the living saints of today.

Second Timothy 1:2-5 and Hebrews 12:1-2 are good scriptures to affirm our celebration of the saints of today and of the past.[1]

SIMPLE EXPLANATION

Years ago, before Christianity spread to many countries, people thought that evil spirits took over the world in the cold and dark months,

so they performed rituals to keep them away. This is the origin of the holiday we call Halloween, October 31. Christians decided to focus on the bright side of the holiday, which tells of Christ and the saints who follow him (both living and dead). These saints make a difference in the world, and we celebrate both dead and living saints like you and me on All Saints' Day, November 1.

LEARNING ACTIVITIES

STUDY SYMBOLS OF APOSTLES

Use page 109 to look at the symbols of the Apostles. Talk about how they were the foundation of our Christian faith.

CREATE A FAITH CREST

Using a shield like those in a family crest, have the children create their own faith crests. On each crest put the child's name with the phrase, "A Saint of God." They may want to draw images on the crest that tell something about themselves and what they do for God.

RESEARCH SAINTS

Check your church or city library for books about persons who have been instrumental to our Christian heritage. The Internet will also have information about some of the people listed below. Some have received formal sainthood from the Roman Catholic Church, while others have not, but they were strong in their faith and are nonetheless saints.

Francis of Assisi—The son of a wealthy man, Francis recognized the problems of the poor and spent his life living in poverty and working with them. He is credited with the first live manger scene at Christmas as he gave those who couldn't read an opportunity to visualize the story. (1181–1226)

Joan of Arc—At age sixteen she heard God calling her to lead the French army against the English invaders. She was successful, disguising herself as a young man, but later the English accused her of witchcraft because she claimed to hear voices from heaven. They burned her at the stake, but she stood firm in her faith (1412–31)

John Wesley—After an unsuccessful time as a missionary to the Americas, he found his heart "strangely warmed" and established small Christian groups called "Classes." The members of these groups had methodical ways to live their lives and were dubbed "Methodists." Wesley insisted on preaching outdoors to the poor, which was unheard of in his day. Wesley later sent preachers, whom he ordained without the approval of the Church of England, to America, and the Methodist Church was born. (1703–91)

Martin Luther—As a Catholic priest in Germany, Martin Luther objected to some of the beliefs of the church. He believed that we can pray to God without going through a priest. He posted his statement of protest on the church door, which began the Protestant Reformation. The Lutheran Church was formed, and other protestant denominations followed. (1483–1546)

Patrick of Ireland—As a young boy, Patrick was taken from his home in England and forced into slave labor in Ireland. He escaped back to England and became a priest. After serving in France for a number of years, he felt a call to returned to Ireland to help those in the same situation that he had endured. He traveled and preached throughout Ireland. He is credited for using the shamrock to describe the Trinity. (387–461)

Teresa of Avila—Known for her practicality and good humor, Teresa combined intelligence and obedience with mysticism. Her writings are appreciated in works of meditation. One of her favorite maxims was that "to give our Lord a perfect service Martha and Mary must combine." (1515–82)

PLAY "ALL SAINTS' DAY"

Assign the following names of saints to the children.

- Francis of Assisi
- Joan of Arc
- John Wesley
- Martin Luther
- Patrick of Ireland
- Teresa of Avila

Form a circle with one less chair than the number of players. Choose the person whose birthday is the closest to today to be "It." Then he or she stands in the middle of the circle and calls out the name of a saint. All those who have that name change places while "It" also tries to get a seat. The person left standing then becomes "It." If "All Saints' Day" is called, everyone changes places.

CREATE A BULLETIN BOARD

Create a bulletin board featuring "Saints of the Past" and "Saints of Today." Include a mirror in the second section.

MAKE A GRAFFITI WALL

Post a large sheet of paper on the wall labeled "Halloween / All Saints' Day." Divide the paper into two sections. On one section write "Without Christ" and on the other write "With Christ." Ask the children to draw pictures of what happens when we live in a world without Christ and in a world with Christ. Talk about the origin of Halloween and All Saints' Day.

CREATE AND USE A LITANY

Using the reproducible on page 11, create a litany of thanksgiving for all saints, both living and dead.

RESEARCH THE WORD SAINT

Use several dictionaries to find the definition of the word *saint*. Using a concordance, look for the use of the word *saint* in both the Old and New Testaments. What are the different ways it is used?

CREATE MONOLOGUES OF SAINTS OF THE PAST

People may dress in costume and tell their story as that character.

INTERVIEW TODAY'S SAINTS

Several weeks ahead of All Saints' Day, interview members of the class and others in the church. Write brief biographies of each person, including why they love God. Put these together in a booklet.

DEMONSTRATE WEAVING

Weaving can remind us that all those who have gone before us have "woven" the fabric of our faith. Ask a weaver to show the children some of the intricacies of weaving. Children can also weave strips of colored paper, naming each one after someone in their past who helped them better understand God.

WORSHIP SUGGESTIONS

USE VISUAL IMAGERY

There are two themes you can use for visual images for this holiday. To emphasize the dark and light sides of the celebration, choose bright and dark objects. To emphasize our heritage with saints of the past and saints of today use:

- roots of a tree—symbolizing those in the past who have been the roots of our faith
- woven cloth—symbolizing how saints of the past and today weave the fabric of our faith
- weaver at a loom—also symbolizing our woven faith

USE HERITAGE BELLS

Use ribbons of bright colors on a standard or a pole. Put a basket of bells on the celebration or worship table and ask each child to select a bell and pin it on a ribbon in memory or in honor of someone who has helped him or her understand God better. As you sing a hymn pass the ribbons from one child to another, listening to the bells that tell of those who set the foundation for our faith.

USE A LITANY

If you created a litany of thanksgiving for all saints (see previous page), use it during worship.

RECITE A SCRIPTURE RESPONSE

Use Psalm 89:15 as a response to a prayer, mentioning saints of the past and present. For an example:

Leader: We thank you, O God, for those who had insight to begin our church in this town.
Response: Blessed are those who have learned to acclaim you, who walk in the light of your presence, O LORD. (NIV)

SING TOGETHER

Use hymns such as those listed below and remind the children that we celebrate all those who follow Christ.

"Faith of Our Fathers" or "Faith of the Martyrs"
"For All the Saints"
"Forward Through the Ages"
"I Sing a Song of the Saints of God"

Thanksgiving

Although our American Thanksgiving holiday is not specifically religious, the act of thankfulness, as an expression to God, is certainly appropriate for a church. The Hebrew heritage of Festival of Tabernacles or Booths can contribute to our celebration. The season should go deeper than simply counting the things we are thankful for.

This is a great opportunity to teach concern for others. Older children can recognize that God does not favor one person above another, and sometimes circumstances cause people to be deprived of the necessities of life. As we are thankful for what we have, we should recognize our obligation to those who are less fortunate than us and do what we can to relieve their problems. Emphasize that our focus at Thanksgiving is more about concern for others than about counting the many privileges we have.

SIMPLE EXPLANATION

Thanksgiving is a special time when we thank God for all of creation, our friends, and opportunities to serve God. It is a time when we can see opportunities to do for others who are not as fortunate as we are.

LEARNING ACTIVITIES

DISTINGUISH BETWEEN "THANKSGIVING" AND "THANKSLIVING"

Ask the children to list things that they are thankful for. Invariably they will list many material things. Continue to ask about which people they are thankful for and opportunities to serve God that they can be thankful for. Then write the word "Thanksliving" on a large sheet of paper or white board. Ask them to list ways that they can express their thankfulness through living out their faith—Thanksliving.

STUDY RUTH

The story of Ruth is believed to have been read at the Hebrew celebration called the Festival of Weeks. The story is an example of a woman who was so thankful for knowing about the one true God that she pledged to go with her mother-in-law into a foreign country, saying, "Your people will be my people and your God my God." (Ruth 1:16 NIV)

CREATE A SUKKAH

A *sukkah* is a booth or open shed with three walls used during the Hebrew harvest as shelter. Help the children create a *sukkah* by lashing poles together and covering the top with branches. Hang fruits and vegetables from the overhead poles. Look at Leviticus 23:42 for the biblical reference to this structure. In later years, the *sukkah* represented the "temporariness" of life on earth. This harvest became an eight-day festival of prayer, feasting, and rejoicing. Because of its symbol of the temporary, the booth is not to be saved from year to year but rebuilt each time. (A quick version of the booth may be made by turning a table upside down and tying poles to the four legs, then lashing poles across the top and adding branches.)

READ THE STORY OF THE TEN LEPERS

Read Luke 17:11-19, the story of the ten men with leprosy whom Jesus healed. Discuss how only one returned to thank Jesus. This broadens our understanding of Thanksgiving to be more than simply thanks for a large meal.

MAKE A THANKSGIVING COLLAGE

Expand your thankfulness by asking the children to draw a special opportunity or surprise that they have had in the past year (for example, a good grade, a surprise visit, or a mission opportunity). Place these in a collage fashion on a bulletin board or a large sheet of paper. Decide as a group on a title for the collage.

LEARN OF THANKSGIVING AROUND THE WORLD

Every country does not celebrate Thanksgiving on the same day as ours, but most countries do have some celebration of thanks. Invite people from other countries to share the customs from their homes or research this in the library or on the Internet.

MAKE STONE SOUP

Invite the children to bring fresh vegetables for stone soup. Begin boiling a big pot of beef or chicken stock with a stone in it that has been scrubbed clean. As you wash and prepare the vegetables, tell the story of

Stone Soup. Below is the outline of the story. Use your storytelling skills to enhance it, but be sure to emphasize the story as an opportunity to share rather than to trick.

> Many years ago in Europe, soldiers entered a town and asked for food. The villagers were afraid and hid their food. The soldiers, however, urged them to share by starting a pot of water boiling and dropping clean stones into the pot. As it boiled, the villagers decided to bring various items from home to share, and soon the whole community was enjoying soup together!

Distribute slices of bread and enjoy the meal. If more food is brought than is needed for the soup, or if there is soup left over, take it to a soup kitchen.

WORSHIP SUGGESTIONS

USE VISUAL IMAGERY

Use the following ideas to create visual imagery in worship:

- items from nature, such as a glass of clear water; fruits of the earth
- pictures or sculptures of people
- symbols of learning institutions
- symbols of caring facilities in your community (such as Habitat for Humanity, hospitals, soup kitchens)

DEDICATE ITEMS OF THANKFULNESS

Ask children to bring items from home that symbolize something they are thankful for. Talk about why they brought specific items, and then place them on a celebration table and say a prayer of thanks for all of them.

OFFER KERNELS OF THANKS

Give each child three kernels of corn. Ask them to name one thing they are thankful for as they put each kernel into a bowl or basket on the celebration table. Then offer thanks to God for each of these kernels of thanks.

Sing Together

Use hymns such as those listed below and remind the children that we celebrate the many blessings we receive from God.

"All Creatures of Our God and King"
"Come Ye Thankful People, Come"
"Holy, Holy, Holy! Lord God Almighty"
"How Great Thou Art"
"Joyful, Joyful, We Adore Thee"
"Let All the World in Every Corner Sing"
"Now Thank We All Our God"
"Praise God, from Whom All Blessings Flow"
"We Gather Together"

MANY ROLES

Sometimes we may feel as if we are many persons. We may be a brother or sister to someone, a child to someone else, a student to still another person. What roles do these people have?

How many roles does your aunt hold?

How many roles does your cousin hold?

How many roles does your mother hold?

How many roles does your grandfather hold?

How many roles do you hold?

Which person had the most titles?
How is each person different to other people?
Does the number of titles make a difference in your relationship to that person?
Does the number of roles make that person that many different people?
How is God like a parent?
How is God like a human being?
How is God like a spirit within us?
How is God like three people?

REPRODUCIBLES

THREE IN ONE

Each year the church celebrates Trinity Sunday. This is when we remember three ways that we understand God. To symbolize this, we often use triangles and other figures with three parts.

In the picture below, see if you can find and circle 20 items that contain three parts.

SYMBOLS OF THE APOSTLES

 **PETER**—The crossed keys recall Peter's confession and our Lord's gift to him of the keys of the kingdom. (See Matthew 16:18-19.)

 **JAMES** (the Lesser)—Represented by a saw, since it is said his body was sawn asunder after a horrible martyrdom.

 **ANDREW**—Tradition says that while Andrew was preaching in Greece he was put to death on a cross of this type.

 **MATTHEW**, as an Apostle—Is symbolized by three purses referring to his original calling as a tax collector.

 **JAMES** (the Greater)—The scallop shell is the symbol of pilgrimage and stands for this apostle's zeal and missionary spirit.

 **THOMAS**—A carpenter's square and a spear, because this apostle is said to have built a church in India with his own hands. Later, he was persecuted there and was killed with a spear by a pagan priest.

 **JOHN**, as an Apostle—Early writers state that John once drank from a poisoned chalice and was unharmed. Jesus once said that John should drink of his cup.

 **BARTHOLOMEW**—This apostle is said to have been flayed alive, hence he is usually represented by three flaying knives.

 **PHILIP**—A cross and two loaves of bread, because of Philip's remark when Jesus fed the multitude. (John 6:7.)

 **SIMON THE ZEALOT**—This symbol is a book upon which rests a fish, because through the power of the gospel Simon became a great fisher of men.

 **JUDE**—This apostle traveled far on missionary journeys in company with Simon, according to tradition, hence the ship.

 **MATTHIAS**—Chosen to take the place of Judas, he is symbolized by an open Bible and double-bladed battle-ax. He is said to have been beheaded after his missionary work.

SUGGESTIONS FOR YOUNGER LEARNERS OR FAMILY EXPERIENCES

In each chapter you will find a brief explanation of the season that is appropriate for younger learners. Young learners can do many of the activities along with older learners or with adults helping them. They can also participate in the worship experiences listed in each chapter. The activities listed below can easily be done by younger learners. They are also appropriate for multiage or family experiences.

Chapter 10—Other Special Days

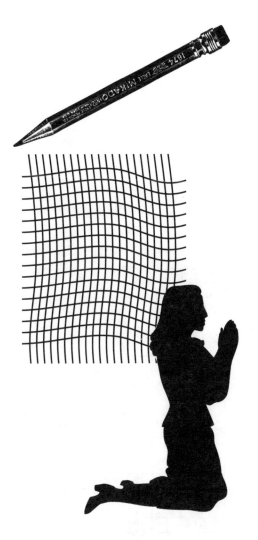

PUZZLE SOLUTIONS

COLORS AND SYMBOLS
OF ADVENT AND CHRISTMAS

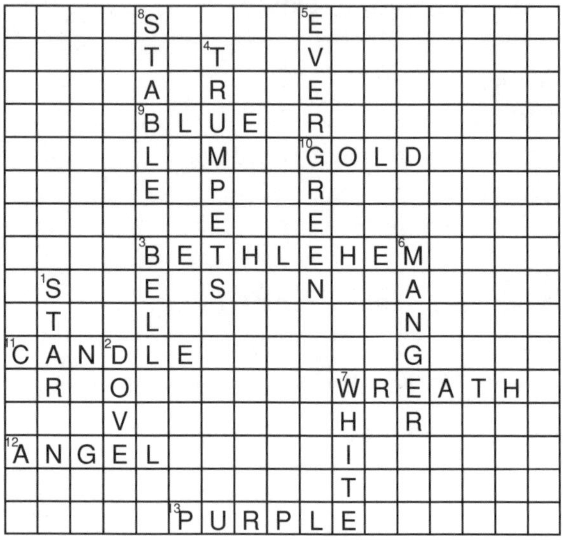

(crossword grid solution)

STABLE, EVERGREEN, TRUE, TRUMPETS, BLUE, GOLD, BETHLEHEM, STAR, BELLS, MANGER, CANDLE, CAROL, ADVENT, WREATH, WHITE, ANGEL, PURPLE

CHAPTER 3

THOSE WHO HELP US WORSHIP

(crossword grid solution)

LITURGIST, DIRECTOR, WORSHIPERS, ORGANIST, PREACHER, USHER, PRAISEBAND, COMMUNIONSTEWARD, CHOIR, GREETER, ALTARGUILD, PRAISETEAM, ACOLYTE, PIANIST

CHAPTER 2

BAPTISM

(crossword grid solution)

PROMISE, WATER, GRACE, POUR, FORGIVENESS, JOHN, JORDAN, BAPTISM, COMMUNION, SACRAMENTS, SPRINKLE, IMMERSE, SHELL, CLEAN

CHAPTER 5

COLORS AND SYMBOLS OF LENT AND EASTER

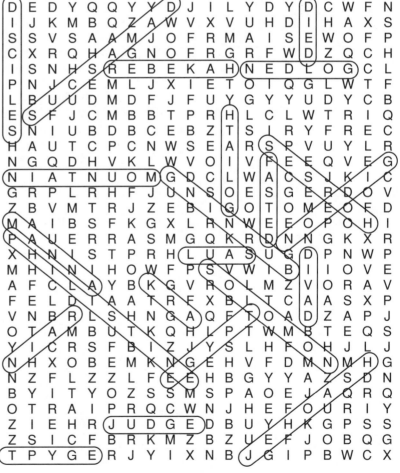

CHAPTER 6

FORTY DAYS

CHAPTER 6

NOTES

1. The Christian Year

1. The drawing is from Marcia Stoner, *Symbols of Faith: Teaching Images of the Christian Faith for Intergenerational Use* (Nashville: Abingdon, 2001), 157.

2. Sundays (Mini-Easters)

1. Portions of this list originally appeared in Delia Halverson, *Teaching Prayer in the Classroom: Experiences for Children and Youth* (Nashville: Abingdon, 1989), 72-73.
2. Delia Halverson, *Helping Children Care for God's People: 200 Ideas for Teaching Stewardship and Mission* (Nashville: Abingdon, 1994), 89.

3. Advent and Christmas

1. This list originally appeared in Delia Halverson, *Teaching and Celebrating the Christian Seasons* (St. Louis: Chalice, 2002), 23-24.

5. Season after Epiphany (Ordinary Time)

1. Delia Halverson, *New Ways to Tell the Old, Old Story: Choosing and Using Bible Stories with Children and Youth* (Nashville: Abingdon, 1992), 31-32.
2. Ibid., 62.

6. Ash Wednesday, Lent, and Holy Week

1. Halverson, *Teaching and Celebrating the Christian Seasons*, 48-49.
2. Ibid., 118-19.

8. Pentecost

1. Halverson, *Teaching Prayer in the Classroom*, 49-50.

9. Season after Pentecost (Kingdomtide)

1. Halverson, *Helping Children Care for God's People*, 62-63.
2. Ibid., 84.
3. Ibid., 66-67.

10. Other Special Days

1. This introduction is from Halverson, *Teaching and Celebrating the Christian Seasons*, 83-84.